Chinese Feast

Christmas

KATHRYN

Kwanza

Hanukkh

Endpaper art by Kathryn Anne Griffin, Marc Laborde, Brian Laborde, Todd Laborde, and John Tracy Laborde—ages two to seven.

Brian

I am thankful for my whole family.

I am thankful for my mom.

La Befana

Fine Tune Your Brain

When Everything's Going Right and what to do when it isn't . . .

Fine Tune Your Brain

When Everything's Going Right
and what to do when it isn't . . .

Written and Illustrated by
Genie Z. Laborde

SYNTONY PUBLISHING
Palo Alto, California

Library of Congress Cataloging-in-Publication Data

Laborde, Genie Z.
    Fine tune your brain.

    Continues: Influencing with integrity.
    Bibliography: p. 261
    Includes index.
    1. Communication in management.
    2. Neurolinguistics.
I. Title.
HD30.3.L32   1988   001.51   87-26723
ISBN 0-933347-30-8 (cloth)
ISBN 0-933347-20-0 (paper)

Printed in the United States of America

Cover design: Tsuneo Taniuchi

Published by
SYNTONY PUBLISHING

1450 Byron Street
Palo Alto, California 94301
10—9—8—7—6—5—4—3—2—1

To John Tracy Laborde, my firstborn, my banker, for supporting me and this book as he moved from secure to entrepreneur

and

to Agnes Waters, my humor editor, without whom I would have lost my sense of.

Other Works by the Author

Influencing with Integrity

Managing Meetings with PEGASUS
    (videotape and workbook)

90 Days to Communication Excellence

Contents

Preface

We have all had those moments when everything was going right. The moments may have lengthened into hours—even days. Then, something shifted, and we were back struggling again—phone calls missed, no parking place, downturns in trends, misunderstandings, frustration, stress. The memory of the time when events flowed smoothly fades and becomes almost unreal.

"When everything's going right" is a phenomenon I have been fascinated with most of my life. I have noticed that people with high energy, with personal power, attracted such moments more often than those with low energy, with lack of presence. So I began to study charismatic, powerful people and the ways in which they functioned.

A sixth century B.C. Chinese philosopher, Lao Tzu, wrote of such personal power in the classic *Tao Te Ching*. He characterized *Te* (pronounced "der") as the potential energy that comes from being in the right place at the right time in the right frame of mind. R. L. Wing tells us, in his translation of the *Tao*: "The early Chinese regarded the planting of seeds as *Te*, and *Te* came to mean stored energy or potentiality." The skills presented in this book will help you release that energy—that power.

As I studied powerful people, I also began to notice how often individuals gave away personal power, sabotaged their own efforts, and seemed to know more about what they did not want than what they did.

People are often stuck in de-energizing patterns. Positive communication energizes; you can tell positive energy people by their bounce. At the end of a business day, the negative energy people are slumping over as they head for the elevator. *Te* is not part of their reality. The opportunity of a lifetime could get on the elevator with them and they would be watching the floor numbers.

To gain the powerful skills of *Te*, most people will need to replace old habit patterns with new patterns. To use the new

=======================================

pattern of *Te*, to be able to respond appropriately in a split-second, takes three steps:

1. Recognize your sabotaging patterns
2. Acquire new options
3. Choose the "right" response at each moment

These three steps require some knowledge of who you are, they require being honest with yourself, and in most cases, they require change. Many people view change as hard work and painful. This is not my experience. I find it exhilarating, energy-producing, and joyful.

Creating moments of everything going right is almost inevitable once you have replaced random responses with the optimum internal states of your choice. This book will tell you how. It is not easy, but it is fun. Enjoy the journey and invite friends to try out these new positive techniques. Once you give them away, they are yours.

As we examine advanced change techniques and their results, we will start with a brief review of skills presented in depth in my earlier book, *Influencing with Integrity*. The summary in Chapter 1 will enable readers who have not read *Influencing* to move through *Fine Tune Your Brain* easily, while offering a quick refresher course to other readers.

I would like to extend my thanks to Brian Berger for the idea for the cartoon on page 78, to Brownie Grey, who told me the story that inspired the illustration on page 120, and to George Flury, whose drawing of the neuron with an axon as well as dendrites inspired the illustration on page 132. Special thanks to my trainers and associates in New York, London, Ottawa, Paris, Milan, Rome, Amsterdam, Johannesburg, Buenos Aires, Melbourne, Stockholm, and New Zealand for their challenges, which keep me on my toes and keep me learning.

And extraordinary thanks to my husband, George, who inspires me to continue to perfect these communication techniques so that a visual-kinesthetic can communicate with an auditory.

Learning to communicate like a master is like learning to ride a bicycle. It takes time and practice for the skills to become automatic.

1
Communication: A Learned Skill

I have a fantasy that one day I will be able to cut my three-day seminars to 30 seconds. In those 30 seconds I would say, "There are three steps to successful communication. The first step is to know what you want. The second step is to find out what the other person wants. The third step is to discover how you both can win. Most of you already have the skills you need. All you have to do is change your words and your behaviors to reflect this philosophy. Oh, yes, and enjoy your interactions." End of seminar.

In 30 seconds the seminar would have accomplished its purpose: to improve the participant's ability to gain acceptance for his/her idea, viewpoint, position. And I would have the reputation for offering the fastest successful seminar in town.

1

Suppose you were using the three steps to successful communication to sell an idea to someone else. This is how the three steps would look.

Step 1. You would know what idea you wanted to sell. You would be aware of this before the communication began.

Step 2. You would find out how your idea, if adopted by the other, would benefit the other. You might have to determine which of the other person's needs your idea could satisfy.

Step 3. If the other person has a need and your idea will help meet it, then dovetailing—matching your outcome and your partner's outcome—is almost certain. If you do not have a perfect fit, you may need to reshape your idea during the interaction until you have a closer match.

For example, suppose you had an idea for an engine that would run on solar energy. You are presenting this idea to an investor, Mr. Bigbucks, who has extra money for venture capital. You need this capital to build a prototype of your engine.

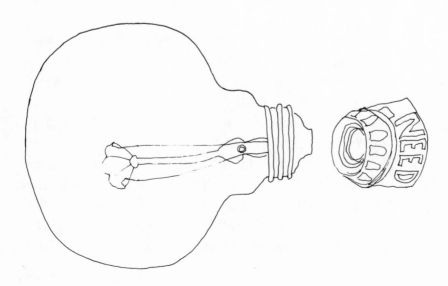

Dovetail—
to set up a
win/win+
agreement

Your first approach might be to demonstrate to Mr. Bigbucks how much money your engine concept will generate. If his need is money and you have rapport based on your credibility, you are well on your way to an agreement. Your outcome and the investor's outcome dovetail.

However, what if Mr. Bigbucks has so much money that he doesn't want any more? Then are you blocked? Are you out the door? What if you uncover the fact that he is ecology-minded and is concerned about automobile emissions and air quality? Then you can begin to dovetail.

Or what if Mr. Bigbucks doesn't care about money or the environment but loves new gadgets? Suppose he has always wanted to market a new product that would make a global impact? You are ready to dovetail.

Here is another example. What if you want to sell the idea of a raise to your boss, Ms. Tightwad? If your boss sees her primary need as keeping expenses down, you do not have a good match immediately. You may want to point out how you could cut office expenses by changing vendors, increasing output, or working extra hours. Perhaps you and other employees are receiving a company benefit that you do not need, and you would rather have its salary equivalent. Maybe you could take over some task Ms. Tightwad hates, such as preparing a monthly budget report. Do something to let your boss know what benefits will result from your salary increase. You may have to be creative to discern the needs of a stingy boss.

Matching idea and need may be the most difficult part of communication, but it is essential. Once need and idea meet, dovetailing is usually very fast and very smooth, as you will see in Chapter 3.

If you cannot think of a way your raise will benefit your boss, my advice is not to ask for one, yet. Invite some friends over, tell them the situation, and brainstorm ways to present your idea so that your boss will recognize the benefit both personally and professionally.

BRAINSTORM

Brainstorming is fun. Simply put your logical mind and your judgmental self on a shelf while you think up all sorts of solutions. Pretend you have a magic wand that erases limitations. After you have collected 20 or 100 farfetched ideas, bring your logical self back, and rate the ideas as to their feasibility.

Take your top three ideas and work out a plan with steps and dates for completing each. Then go for it.

A SKILLS SET

The basic and advanced skills you will learn in this book evolved from a discipline called "paralinguistics," or "neurolinguistics," or "syntonics"—the study of all parts of communication, not just language. This discipline is being taught at universities (e.g., Stanford Graduate School of Business, UCLA, Vanderbilt University, and John F. Kennedy University), and it is now impacting business in areas such as banking (Chase Manhattan), telecommunications (AT&T), utilities (Florida Power & Light Co.), and computers (IBM).

is paralinguistics or neurolinguistics applied to business.

Most of us have mastered the "left-brain" communication skills—understanding the words spoken—but many of us are not aware of the "right-brain" skills and lack the ability to understand the total communication conveyed by facial changes, gestures, skin color shifts, voice tones, and body posture. Communication experts have shown that these aspects of communication are as important, if not more so, than the words being exchanged. The whole gestalt (pattern) of communication carries significant additional information for persons who have learned to fine-tune their perceptions to pick up this rich other "language."

The communication skills presented in this book are derived from studies of the way sensory data are organized in your memory banks. As you become more adept at using your five senses, new and useful thinking skills emerge, and you become more successful in controlling the communication process. Here are ten skills that will fine-tune your communication interactions.

Skill 1: Know What You Want

Before you begin to communicate, you must decide what you want to accomplish. What you want, the goal of your communication, is your outcome. To turn a goal into an outcome takes thinking in a certain way—thinking that employs sensory-based information.

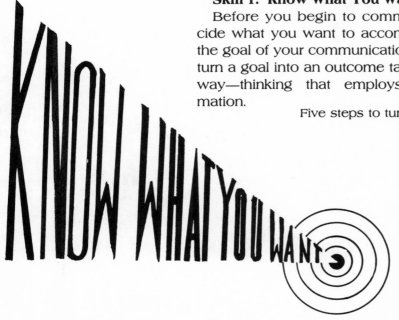

Five steps to turn a goal into an outcome:

A Aim for a specific result;

B Be positive—express outcomes in terms of *doing* rather than *not doing*;

C *See, hear,* and *feel*—use sensory data;

D Dovetail your desires with those of your communication partner;

E Entertain short- and long-term objectives.

**Skill 2: Know Your Preferred Sense and
Learn Your Partner's**

Our five senses collect "sensory" data—they see, hear, feel, smell, and taste as they collect information from the world around us. These senses and their data begin the communication process, guide it, and determine how we behave. Each of us trusts, esteems, and utilizes the data from one sense more than the data from the other senses. We each prefer one sense and its information to perceive, to think, and to select our words. This means that some of us prefer pictures, some prefer sounds, and some prefer feelings to "make sense" of the world we live in. (Because smells and tastes are less important in communication than the input from our other senses, in this book they are included in the kinesthetic, or "feeling," sense.)

We thus have three categories of people speaking different languages even while speaking English. Visuals use a lot of "see" expressions, such as "I get the picture," "I see what you mean," or even "I see what you are saying." Auditories may say, "I like the sound of that" or "That rings a bell." Kinesthetics like words such as "feel," "grasp," and "handle." They may say, "I feel we're moving right along" or "I've got a handle on that."

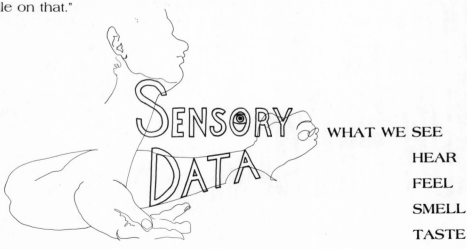

WHAT WE SEE

HEAR

FEEL

SMELL

TASTE

Visuals

Auditories

Kinesthetics

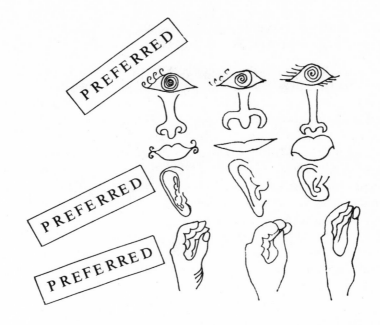

This is more important than you would think.

People who store most of their memory information in pictures are called visuals.	People who prefer sound memories are auditories.	People who prefer memories of feelings, smells, and tastes are kinesthetics.

An excellent communicator needs to recognize which language is being spoken and to match that language for improved understanding. If you do not "translate" for another, you risk a loss of rapport and miscommunication. You can deepen understanding by taking the time to listen to the sensory words your partner is using. Then you can select words from his/her favorite perceptual system to reply. This takes some practice, but the time is well spent.

You will increase your understanding of others when you begin to translate, and your own language will become more colorful. You will also notice some surprising changes in your ability to understand your partner's communication.

Skill 3: Enhance Rapport by Matching Your Partner's Voice and Breathing Rate

Before you can communicate effectively with anyone, you must establish a feeling of trust, or rapport. In business, rapport is based on trust in competence for the task in which the two of you are engaged. Rapport usually occurs when two people find a common ground. While you are locating this common ground, matching your partner's voice is one way to accelerate rapport. You do not need to match exactly; a slight shift is all that is necessary.

All of us speak in a certain habitual way. We have a loud voice, a slow voice, a fast voice, a soft voice, which we have acquired through years of communicating. We are mostly unaware of our voice pattern. Yet, if you pay attention to the pattern of your communication partner's voice, especially the rhythm, you can subtly match his/her voice, and this will often establish rapport. The other person will become more comfortable with you. The common ground you have established is voice matching, which in itself results in matching breathing rate. Breathing and voice rhythms are intertwined. When people match breathing rhythms, a sense of common ground often occurs naturally, and this is usually enough to establish rapport.

The one thing that will interfere with rapport here is if one or the other plans to "take advantage." Manipulation assumes many forms, and manipulative thinking will block rapport. Going into an interaction with the idea of finding a win/win+ solution for both of you encourages rapport as you seek a common ground.

Some people find breathing rates difficult to identify and match. If this is the case with you, try voice matching, and you will find you are probably matching breathing rates as well.

Skill 4: Check Your Partner's Preferred Sense by Watching Eye Movements

Many of you are familiar with the way eye movements indicate a person's primary sense: visuals tend to look up for stored pictures; auditories move their eyes left and right, about midline, and down left; kinesthetics look down to their right. When you become aware of your partner's primary sense, you can adjust your language to choose more appropriate and meaningful words. For example, if your communication partner looks up a lot, try visual questions such as, "Do you have a clear picture of my proposal?" A question for auditories, who will be recalling memories stored in sounds and words, would be, "How does this sound to you?" And you might want to ask a kinesthetic, who is primarily interested in sensation, "What's your feeling about this?"

When you are communicating with others, notice where they move their eyes. Up or defocused is to find pictures, down and to the right is for feelings, and all other eye movements are for sounds or words. You can determine whether people are visual, auditory, or kinesthetic by noticing which eye movements they use most often. People must move their eyes to find stored memories, and these eye movements reveal their preferred sense.

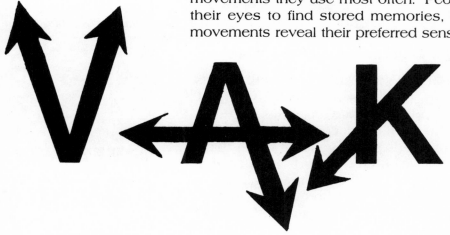

Skill 5: Develop Sensory Acuity—Sensory Awareness Carried One Step Further

Sensory acuity takes you a step beyond awareness so that you are better at seeing and hearing than most communicators. So much is going on when two people are communicating that much of it does not register. Most people simply hear some of the words and notice a passing expression. You can train yourself to notice all kinds of unconscious visible responses during a conversation. And once you have done this, you will have greater insight into what the other is saying—and not saying.

Four responses to notice in a communication are subtle skin color changes, small facial muscle reactions, lower lip changes, and breathing rate fluctuations. When you notice these in others, pay attention to the feelings that go along with them. Remember, of course, that one person may breathe quickly when excited, another when angry, another when anxious. These physical signs are only signals that a change has taken place. You will have to use your other skills to determine the meaning of the response.

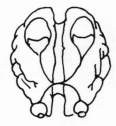

Each time you learn something new, you change your neurology.

Skill 6: Use Questions to Clarify Vague Words

We have focused on some of the nonverbal parts of communication; now it is time to listen to the words—to go beyond the surface meanings of certain classes of words to learn the deeper meanings.

Certain types of words signal you that better thinking and more information are needed. Recognizing significant but vague words in a communication and asking clarifying questions will shorten your interactions and make them more productive. Significant words are usually important nouns, verbs, rules, and generalizations. By asking questions about these, you can clarify and simplify what people are saying.

To eliminate misunderstanding caused by vague words, begin to speak in precise terms—use words that are closely related to see, hear, and feel information. Instead of telling someone you want a report on a project next week, you might say, "I want to see five or six pages of action steps that will implement your project by September 15. Do include personnel, budget costs, and time frame to begin." Or you might say, "Give me a verbal report with several options, so we can determine which is the most appropriate, next Tuesday at 2 o'clock." If you give explicit instructions, your staff will know what to do. If you use vague words, they may be successful at guessing what you want, but probably not.

When you hear an important noun in someone else's communication, you will do well to ask *what* and *how* questions. For example:

Employee: "I do not like this project."
Employer: "*What* kind of project would you like?"
Employee: "One that I felt was significant."
Employer: "*How* would you know that a project was significant?"

Four Super Questions:
1. What?
2. How?
3. What would happen if?
4. All?

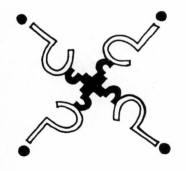

"Project," and "significant" have many meanings, and until you know each other's meaning, neither of you can effectively move toward the goal. When the other person can tell you how "significant" looks, sounds, and feels, then you have moved toward clarifying the communication.

As another example, a manager might say, "We have to be more cost-effective." "More cost-effective" could mean many different things. This statement does not help the staff know how their behavior should change. Either the subordinates or the boss should clarify what "more cost-effective" would look like, sound like, feel like.

Subordinates often receive too little information on projects that have many possible action options. As a result, they may select the option that is the least useful for the person in charge.

A certain category of words establishes rules, and people often accept these rules without questioning their limiting qualities. Words like "must," "must not," "have to," "cannot," and "ought to" eliminate other behavior options, and new behavior options can be ways to solve problems.

Consider this rule: "All employees must work from 8 a.m. to 5 p.m." Suppose Tom, an employee in accounting, could carpool if he left at 4:30. After gaining rapport, he might ask, "I'm wondering if you would be willing to tell me why we all have to be here from 8 a.m. to 5 p.m.? What would happen if I come in at 7:30?"

Coming in earlier might have advantages that had not been thought of when the 8 to 5 rule was drafted. Tom might be able to get assignments ready for the data processing group or make important long distance calls if he started each day a half hour earlier. Rules limit behaviors, often in ways that are not productive. Sometimes the rules have been in place for so long that no one remembers the original purpose. By exploring with a "What would happen if . . ." question, you may discover new and stimulating alternatives. Think of the effect such questions have had in the past: "What would happen if we sailed west, to the edge of the earth?" "What would happen if we built a machine to fly?"

Words such as "always," "all," "never," "everybody," and "they" alert you that generalization is at work. You may already recognize these generalizations. Challenging them is the next important step. So when you hear a generalization such as, "That group never produces," ask, "Never?" Then, perhaps, you will discover conditions under which the group does deliver.

Generalizations often reflect sloppy thinking, which costs money, time, and effort. By spotting the generalizations in your own and your colleagues' thinking patterns, you can begin to use language to help you solve problems. In the one exception to the rule may lie the answer to a problem.

Another group of vague words to watch for are comparisons that lack antecedents. People often use "better," "more," and "best" to compare situations, people, and things. When you hear sentences like, "He's the best" or "That division produces better," you will find it useful to ask, "Best compared to whom?" or "Better compared to what?" Comparisons without antecedents are a sign that more thinking skills are in order.

By becoming aware of vague words and learning to question them, you will make your language more precise and you will be able to clarify imprecise language in others. Precise questions elicit precise information and eliminate a lot of misunderstanding.

Skill 7: Conduct Short Meetings with High-Quality Outcomes

P *Present outcome visually*

E *Evidence*

G *Gain agreement on outcomes*

A *Ask each person*

S *Sensory acuity*

U *Use relevancy challenge*

S *Summarize, and specify next step*

The meeting format PEGASUS provides an opportunity to use the preceding skills, and one or two new skills as well. By using this format and your communication skills, you can eliminate the biggest problem with meetings: nonproductive time. PEGASUS, which appears in detail in *Influencing with Integrity*, outlines the steps to a productive meeting. Here is a quick review:

Present your outcome visually. Use a chalkboard or a flip chart so everyone can see the outcome.

Evidence. Choose the criteria to be used as evidence that the meeting outcome has been met.

Gain agreement on outcome. It is important to ask each person to agree to the outcome presented and to the evidence that will determine whether that outcome has been realized.

Ask each person. The leader of the meeting can ask each person if s/he agrees with the written outcome. This move ensures that the relevancy challenge will be observed.

Sensory acuity. Use your improved sensory awareness, your sensory acuity, to discover any hidden agenda meeting participants may have.

Use relevancy challenge. By challenging irrelevant comments, you can keep the meeting on track and save valuable time. Because you have already gained everyone's agreement on the meeting's outcome, you can question extraneous statements politely, "How is that relevant?" This technique is one of the most effective you can use.

Summarize, and specify next step. When the outcome has been reached, as demonstrated by the evidence, then a final summary is in order, along with the next step each person present is to take.

PEGASUS will cut your meeting time by 30% and give you high-quality outcomes.

Skill 8: Unblock Conflicts

Negotiations become blocked when two or more people cannot agree. This is when you need some new ways to think about the situation. If you ask each of the parties the intention behind a demand, new information may turn up to unblock the negotiation. For example, if two colleagues want the same new office and do not want to share it, new thinking skills are needed. You could say, as manager, "Tell me, Mr. X, what would it mean to you to have this particular office?"

He might reply, "My present office is so noisy that I find it difficult to concentrate. I could work better in a quiet office." The intention behind Mr. X's demand is the need for a quieter workplace.

Then you might ask Mr. Z more about his demand for the office. He might say, "My office is inside and doesn't have a window. I get depressed working under fluorescent lights all day." The intention behind Mr. Z's demand is to work in daylight.

Now you have other options available. The new office may not be the only possible solution. Mr. Z might be willing to share a big office if it has windows, and Mr. X might move to any office that is quiet. By finding out intentions, you may discover creative ways to solve an apparent conflict.

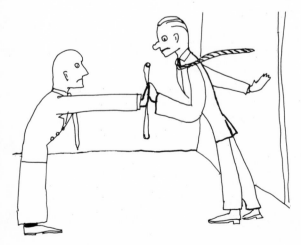

Four words to unblock
any conflict:

WHAT

DO

YOU

WANT?

Skill 9: Flexibility

For many people the ability to be flexible is inhibited by their "character." The word "character" has two meanings: (1) attributes that distinguish us from one another; (2) moral excellence and firmness. The two meanings sometimes overlap in our thinking—we begin to believe that if we change our attributes, we abandon our moral excellence. By separating the two meanings, we can change our attributes and be flexible while retaining our moral fiber.

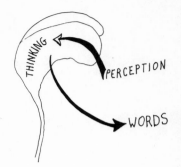

In our culture, persons with "character" are often perceived as stable, consistent, and predictable and are admired for these qualities. Those admiring are often comforted by the reassuring "sameness" of behavior exhibited by those with "character."

The problem with "sameness" is that events are changing around us, and flexibility is necessary to behave appropriately in a changing world. Many people are stranded with behaviors that no longer work to gain their outcomes.

Awareness that what you are doing is not working for you is the first step toward flexibility. The second step is to find an appropriate alternative behavior. Finding and using new behaviors will require flexibility and congruence.

Skill 10: Congruence

Congruence is the way to make your words heard, to develop your personal power. When you are congruent, your client, customer, boss, and staff will listen carefully. The search for congruence involves some interesting internal journeys, which you will take in later chapters. Congruence is so important for successful communication that it is the subject of a separate chapter (Chapter 6, Communicating Congruently).

Once you have acquired the basic skills set, you will be ready to move on—you will be ready for advanced communication skills. Fine-tuning your brain becomes automatic with these skills.

ADVANCED SKILLS IN
COMMUNICATION AND SELF-KNOWLEDGE

As you read through this book, you will find advanced skills—skills that will enable you to communicate effectively, even in difficult situations. You will learn how your brain learns, how it is programmed, and how to reprogram and fine-tune it to a high level of performance. You will learn, specifically, how to dovetail (Chapter 3), how to recognize and deal with negative communication patterns (Chapter 4), how to construct metaphors to enhance communication (Chapter 5), how to change an unwanted behavior (Chapter 7), how to create a resource state (Chapter 9), how to "change history" (Chapter 11), and how to erase fears (Chapter 12).

Once you have mastered these thinking and behavioral skills, you will need to be very careful about which approaches you select. A fine-tuned brain is an awesome instrument.

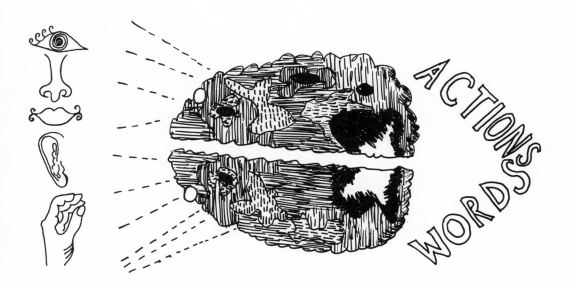

Brain maps of positron-emission transaxial tomography

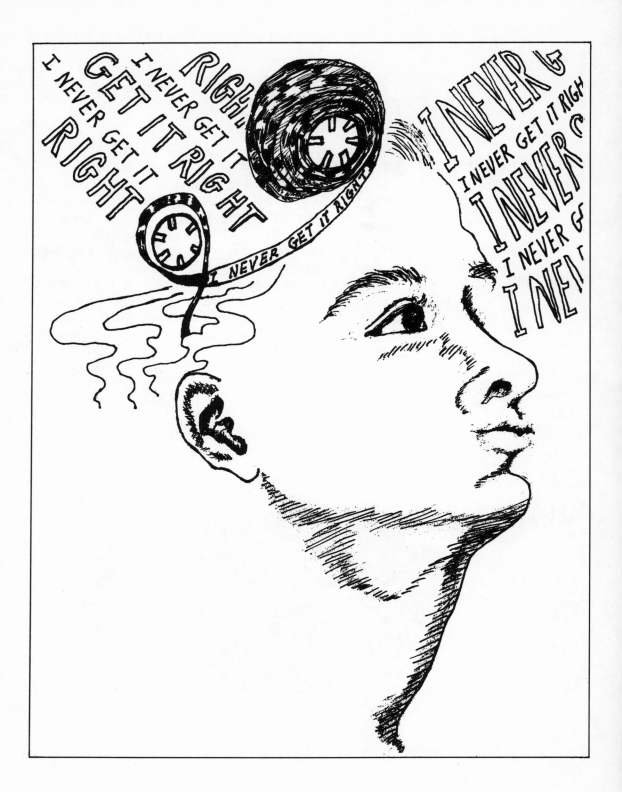

2
Three Quickskills

Being in the right frame of mind is a shortcut to the many avenues of success in business communication. Usually, *what* you say is less important than *how* you say it. The *how* is determined by your frame of mind— your internal state.

You can learn how to put yourself in the most appropriate internal state for your outcome during any interaction and how, if necessary, to change internal states several times. It is important to know that you can change any internal state whenever you wish. Anytime you feel angry, insecure, or pessimistic, you can *choose* to feel peaceful, confident, and optimistic instead. On the other hand, now you cannot blame anyone else for your bad "moods."

Many people find it difficult to believe that an internal state—a feeling of depression (a "grey cloud") or lack of confidence—can be changed to another internal state by a specific series of steps. Even those who know that they can change internal states hesitate to use the skill; they tend to save it for "special" occasions. There is nothing magical or metaphysical about changing states, although the effects may seem extraordinary. Many cultures have known about this skill, but it was often hidden in rituals that obscured the simplicity of the process.

Our joys, our broken hearts, our angers, our creative impulses are reflections of electrochemical patterns that move across the brain. Once Ivan Pavlov discovered the principle of stimulus-response (which we will explore further in Chapter 8), he demonstrated that these brain patterns are susceptible to intervention. You can change your patterns—your habits of thinking. You can switch internal states. Before you make that sales call or ask your boss for a raise, you can put yourself in your best internal state.

I do not know why it has taken us so long to figure this out. Part of the problem may be that no one wants to believe that changing his/her bad moods is that simple. The thinking goes something like this: "Other people's moods may succumb to 'tricks' like this, but my moods have depth—real depth. No tricks will work on them."

But the brain sets up its electrically channeled patterns as smoothly and efficiently for positive states as it does for negative ones. The brain will produce euphoria or contentment or pride or confidence or depression or pessimism or whatever you wish, depending on the perceptions you put into it to act as stimuli for your own personalized responses. It is in the area of these "personalized responses" that the freedom to switch your internal state exists. You can orchestrate these responses. You learned them originally; now you can learn new responses and replace the ones you dislike.

Internal States

Here are some examples of internal states that you may have experienced or noticed in others:

By-the-book/Creative

One down/Equal

Relaxed/Tense

Insecure/Confident

Scattered/Focused

Disdainful/Respectful

Lethargic/Alert

Enthusiastic/Dispirited

Peaceful/Angry

Pessimistic/Optimistic

Responsive/Bland

Playful/Grave

Humble/Proud

Indecisive/Decisive

Unconcerned/Concerned

Structured/Spontaneous

Flexible/Rigid

Agitated/Calm

Perceptions are the see, hear, and feel sensory data we gather from our environment.

SNAKE OIL

Lose Weight Easily
End Stomach Problems
Erase Wrinkles
Stop Asthma Attacks
End Backaches
Cure Irregular Menstruation
Stop Smoking
Eliminate Nervous Tension

When I read what I had written in this chapter, my skeptical self whispered, "Snake oil. You sound like those ads for a cure-all."

My skeptical self has served me well—protected me from many potential disasters. I encourage your skepticism as well. Do not believe any of these claims until you try the techniques and they work. Your "personalized responses" have been running efficiently and smoothly for a long time, so changing them will take some attention and persistence. Some people can change their patterns rapidly once they understand how; only a few are unsuccessful. This book will give you the information you need to change your patterns at the neurological level.

Three fairly simple processes, demonstrated in three mental exercises later in this chapter, can eliminate some negative patterns you may have laid down in your brain. Do not be deceived by the simplicity of these three exercises; each is powerful in changing behaviors that may be decreasing or sabotaging your effectiveness. The exercises will show you mental skills that may surprise you. We are only now beginning to learn how to exercise our brains.

CHANGING INTERNAL STATES

Do any of these comments sound familiar?

- "I never get it right."
- "This is my one big chance."
- "I'm going to screw this up. I know it."
- "This is out of my league."
- "I can't handle this alone. I need help."
- "He's going to say 'no.' I can hear it now."
- "Cold calls don't work for me."
- "I'm wearing the wrong thing."
- "This presentation won't work with this group."
- "Why does this always happen to me?"

If you use tension to keep you alert and flexible, fine. A little tension is like a little stage fright. Veteran actors know that slight stage fright will "rev" them up to give their best performance. A little tension can be useful to bring your full attention to a crucial situation. But excessive tension—being extremely uptight or anxious—will have a negative effect on your interactions. Deep-seated anxiety cannot be concealed by loud words, smiles, or jovial behavior. It expresses itself in unconscious gestures, facial expressions, and body postures that communicate clearly to your partner on a subliminal, if not on a conscious, level. The resulting discomfort your partner feels will probably lead to a rejection of whatever proposal you make—from "Let's have lunch" to "Let's sign the contract today." Anxiety will usually trigger caution, delay, and perhaps rejection, no matter how good your product, your sales pitch, or your expertise. Whenever possible, smart business people avoid those who are anxious. Since subliminal anxiety *is* contagious, why do business with someone who is spreading it?

CHECK YOUR STATE

Could you be transmitting anxiety through unconscious signals and not know it? How do you find out?

Ask a friend or colleague who will level with you. If the answer to the question "Do I seem to be tense?" is "yes," then you need to learn two skills: first, to control your auditory tapes and, second, to access a resource state at any time. In this chapter you will learn the quickskill of turning down your negative auditory tapes. In Chapter 9, you will learn how to access a resource state—a state of excellence in which all your life resources are available to you.

The first step in controlling your internal tapes, those auditory put-downs—such as "I never get it right" —is to turn them off, or at least turn them down.

A sprinkle of ANXIETY

QUICKSKILL 1: HOW TO CONTROL
NEGATIVE AUDITORY TAPES

This exercise will teach you how to handle internal auditory tapes that are giving you negative messages and, perhaps, causing tension. Because you want to be at your best in communication interactions, you do not want a negative voice inside saying you are doing it all wrong. So let's quiet that voice. You need to be alone to do this exercise because the behaviors will look peculiar to anyone watching you. The entire process should take no longer than a minute or two.

First, listen for negative internal words and sentences until you hear them clearly. Then pretend you have a radio in front of you. Actually reach out your hand and turn an imaginary dial until the internal tapes *increase* in volume. Listen to be sure the voices in your head become louder. Enjoy your control.

Now reach out and turn down the sound of your internal tapes on that imaginary radio until you notice that the voices are lower. Continue to lower the sound until it is like the distant murmur of the ocean. The sound is still there, but you can no longer distinguish the words. The distant murmur may even be soothing.

OCEAN WAVES
    MURMUR

This soothing sound, which can replace messages
such as "I never get it right," will be useful in creating
successful communication interactions. Replacing
your negative sounds with positive sounds (the murmur of the ocean, the song of birds, the wind playing
in the leaves of mountain birches, or whatever sound
you choose) will reduce tension and improve your
performance.

One nice thing about emotional states is that opposite states cannot cohabit. For example, tension and
relaxation are incompatible. You can move from one
state (tension) to another state (relaxation) by changing anxiety-producing sounds to relaxing sounds. If
you are listening to soothing sounds, you will feel
soothed—not tense; your internal feelings will change.
Perhaps you want to feel alert, as well as relaxed,
during an interaction. Alertness and relaxation are
not opposites, so the two feelings can be combined,
whereas relaxation and tension cannot.

Relaxation with curiosity is a positive state for me. I often replace tension with relaxed curiosity. If you can remember a sound that reminds you of relaxed curiosity (mine is being in bed with a good book and hearing the sound of a car starting up not too far away), then replace your negative auditory sounds with that memory. Try it. Controlling negative auditory tapes is one of several techniques you can use to change internal states. People have organized their brain processes in different ways, and one technique may be more effective for some than for others. Changing your internal tapes may not be the best way for you to change your internal state. However, the exercise takes only a minute or two, so I recommend you try it. Later in this chapter you will learn two other techniques for changing states, and later in the book you will be introduced to some advanced change strategies.

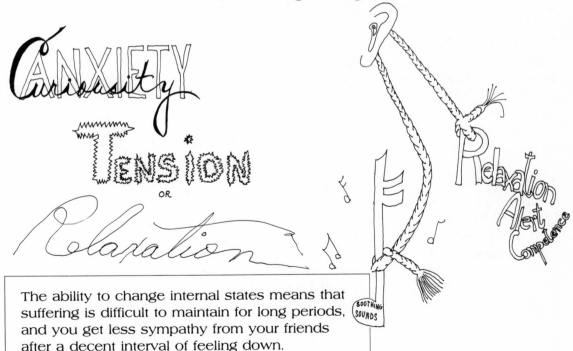

The ability to change internal states means that suffering is difficult to maintain for long periods, and you get less sympathy from your friends after a decent interval of feeling down.

Check Your Energy Levels

Before we go on to quickskill 2, I want you to do a preliminary exercise. First, think about listening to someone blaming you for something you did or did not do. Listen carefully to the person's words, to the tone of voice; then pay attention to your feelings. How do you feel? Circle one number below and record your energy level.

Energy—vigor or power in action

ENERGY LEVEL

Low   0   1   2   3   4   5   6   7   8   9   10   HIGH

Now quickly remember a specific time when someone told you how glad s/he was to see you and how great you looked. Remember how that person's expression, posture, and all his/her behaviors reflected the words. You knew you looked great to that person. See that person looking at you approvingly, hear the words, and recall the feeling of acceptance. How do you feel? Record your energy level by circling one number.

ENERGY LEVEL

Low   0   1   2   3   4   5   6   7   8   9   10   HIGH

Now think about spending time with a complainer. Listen to that person's complaints. Then switch to another person who complains and listen again. Finally, think of one more complainer, and listen carefully until you have an internal response to these three voices. Now how do you feel? Circle one number.

ENERGY LEVEL

Low   0   1   2   3   4   5   6   7   8   9   10   HIGH

Recall a time recently when you discovered a new idea that would be useful in your life. Maybe you came across the idea in a book, heard it on your car radio, or got it from a friend. You may even have discovered the idea in school. Now remember the excitement of playing around with a new piece of knowledge. How do you feel? Circle one number.

ENERGY LEVEL

Low   0   1   2   3   4   5   6   7   8   9   10   HIGH

Can you remember interacting with a person who justifies all his/her actions? Perhaps you sat next to someone like this on a plane or you work with one. Or maybe one married into your family, and you have those Thanksgiving dinners and Christmas holidays to listen to all those justifications. Think of one of those conversations, and record your energy level. Circle one number.

ENERGY LEVEL

Low   0   1   2   3   4   5   6   7   8   9   10   HIGH

Have you ever gotten an unexpected raise or bonus? Received an award? Won a scholarship? Won a contest of any kind? Been recognized by your boss for doing an outstanding job? How did you feel in the middle of being recognized for outstanding behavior? Record that energy level.

ENERGY LEVEL

Low   0   1   2   3   4   5   6   7   8   9   10   HIGH

Now look at your pattern of energy level fluctuations, and note which interactions raise your energy level and which lower it. Most of us wake up in the morning with a bucket of energy. Some of us fill the bucket during the day. Whether you are a morning person or an evening person, sometimes you have high energy, and other times you have low energy. Did you ever wonder why? At least part of the reason for the fluctuation lies in negative interactions with people who lower your energy by blaming, complaining, and justifying. "Dumping" is another term for this pattern. Here is a clever way to raise your own energy level and that of your "dumping" communication partner.

QUICKSKILL 2: HOW TO SCRAMBLE COMMUNICATION FOR INCREASED ENERGY

Do you have a client, colleague, or employee who sorts through his/her daily experiences and selects all the negative ones to "share" with you? Most of us slip into this behavior now and then. Exploring our negative emotional experiences seems to help alleviate some of the frustration and pain.

There are people—you may know some—who have a pattern of negative communication. Their constant recital of problems and woes can drain the energy level of all within earshot. The next time someone begins dumping unhappy experiences on you, here is an antidote—a way to alleviate the negative feelings, and possibly shift them to positive ones.

This antidote has six steps: (1) "Hear out" the negative experience. By listening carefully, you will probably gain rapport. (2) Select the key words of the experience as expressed by the other person. (3) Say, "Tell me about the best thing that has happened to you today" (or "this week," "this month"—in extreme

"Let's share"

cases, "your life"). Encourage a full description, complete with pictures, sounds, and feelings. (4) Select the key positive words. (5) Weave the two experiences (good and bad) together by using both positive and negative key words. Keep checking on rapport. (6) Continue weaving good and bad elements until you notice a response toward the positive in physical appearance and voice tone. Now, let's explore these steps in more detail.

A Scramble

Listen to the negative experience or experiences. As you listen, begin to establish rapport. You might try matching gestures, tone, and breathing rate. You will need rapport before you can scramble.

Select the key words of the negative experience. People mark key words or phrases by extra emphasis and, often, by pauses in front of the key words and phrases. As they talk, they "highlight" certain words, just as yellow markers do in books. With a little practice in tuning your ear, you can note these key words for later use, when you begin to weave the positive and negative elements.

Ask the other person to tell you about a positive experience. Before you can ask for this, you must have enough rapport for the person to shift out of the negative memory and begin to search for a positive experience. If you know the person well enough, you may be able to prompt a memory of a positive experience. You may need to lead the person by saying, "Your story reminds me of a time. . . ." Then relate a negative experience that turned out to be positive in the long run. After this, you can gracefully ask the person for a good experience. If s/he is unable to recall a positive experience, you may need to make some suggestions.

Select the key words from the positive experience.
Selecting key words and phrases is a skill you will find useful in many communication interactions, and it is easy to learn. By shifting your attention to key words, you will become more skillful at eliminating the "fluff" that disguises important ideas. When you eliminate the fluff, you free your auditory track to record the important content. Once you have the key words and phrases, you are ready to begin scrambling.

The unimportant connecting words that often hide the real communication. The best examples are heard in college classrooms.

Begin to weave (scramble) positive and negative experiences. You might start by saying something like this:

"You sound as *frustrated (angry, confused, upset)* talking about the *project (assignment, job, report)* now as you did when you started the X *project* three years ago. Remember how *frustrated (angry, confused, upset)* you felt at the beginning of that *project (assignment, job, report)* and then how *excited (enthusiastic, calm, pleased, satisfied)* you felt when the *project (assignment, job, report)* was completed successfully?"

If you already know of a previous experience that will compare smoothly with the current one, you can move the person quickly through the Scramble.

Or you may have to "wing it"—just begin to weave the positive and negative key words together with enough fluff to appear logical. Actually, if you have indeed selected the key words, the other person will be so responsive and caught up in the emotions around the key words that s/he will probably not notice what you are doing.

Even though this is a new behavior on your part, as long as you remain relaxed and attentive, the other person will probably go along with your "weaving," no matter how transparent your fluff. One reason is that, after a few sentences, the other person will

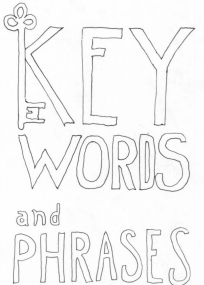

carry the important information.

begin to feel better and will be encouraged to hear you out. Another reason is that we each tend to organize what we hear to fit our own presuppositions. Therefore, even if you are an apprentice weaver, the other person may organize the gist of the communication into whatever pattern s/he expects from you, without really noticing your stops and starts and unusual communication patterns.

Continue weaving (scrambling) until you notice a positive physiological shift. This shift may be observable in facial expression, body posture, and voice tone—even when negative key words are being used. This part of the Scramble can take five minutes or, in some cases, much longer.

Strategy for a Scramble

Fluff fluff negative fluff fluff positive then fluff negative fluff positive then negative positive positive negative negative negative positive positive then negative positive negative positive. (Note physical shift. Congratulate yourself.)

What about the effect of the other person's negative communication on you? Negative words do affect us, and the best way to neutralize them is to scramble the communication. As it works for the speaker, it will work for you as well. When we are communicating, we are in a feedback system. Our impact on one another is much greater than we realize.

I taught the Scramble to a group of students at a university after about ten hours of class time. One student, Paul, tried it with another student that night, beginning about 10 p.m. They completed the exercise at 12:30 a.m., but were so energized by the positive emotions generated and so surprised at the efficacy of shuttling back and forth from positive to negative that they talked for hours.

Paul decided to try the exercise with one of his employees. Here is Paul's account, with the employee's name changed.

Paul's Scramble

Within a few days after the first class session, I saw an opportunity to use the Scramble exercise with one of my employees. Although Gary is a highly valued employee and an exceptionally diligent and hardworking laborer, he spends most of his free time at work telling the rest of us how miserable his domestic life is. His vivid descriptions of his anguish have a tendency to lower the morale of the whole crew. On one occasion I actually sent him home shortly after he arrived because his presence on the job would certainly have negatively affected both the quality and the productivity of our work.

During a morning coffee break, Gary began to deliver his ongoing saga of personal unhappiness. Rather than try to change the subject, as I usually did, I listened attentively, observing Gary's facial expression and body posture and noticing the key phrases he used to emphasize his unhappy situation. Before the break was over, I asked if he would like to help me with one of my homework assignments, and he agreed. I invited him to join me after work for a beer at one of his favorite "watering holes."

After we sat down at a corner table, I gave Gary a brief description of my assignment and got his permission to participate. I quickly called to mind the various techniques I had considered using since this opportunity had first presented itself at the morning coffee break.

Without overdoing body-mirroring, I took a position similar to his by stretching out my legs and crossing my ankles, resting my arm on the back of

Body-mirroring is duplicating someone else's posture to establish rapport. This can backfire and break rapport.

Restraint in body-mirroring is important in setting up rapport. A little goes a long way.

an adjacent chair, and holding my glass of beer in one hand. This effort seemed quite helpful in establishing rapport. I then asked Gary to tell me about the worst experience he'd had in the last few days. In less than a minute he was fully involved in describing the details of his domestic doldrums. I observed his breathing pattern and did my best to synchronize my breathing in order to further develop rapport.

> Matching someone else's breathing helps in establishing rapport as long as you are dovetailing.

A visual orientation means Gary prefers pictures over sounds and feelings to make sense of his world.

His eye movements suggested a visual orientation, and his hand/arm gestures coincided with certain key phrases and vocal emphasis in tone and tempo. After several minutes, having developed a pretty good sense of the experience he was communicating, I faced the problem of shutting him up. I remembered the suggested techniques for breaking rapport, and I quickly turned toward the bar and loudly ordered another round. Rapport was sufficiently sundered.

> A sudden abrupt movement or interruption may break rapport.

As we hoisted a toast to our second round, I used the toasting gesture to begin reestablishing rapport. I asked Gary to describe his best experience within the last few days; he merely returned a dull glance. I did some mirroring and breath synchronizing to deepen rapport, but these did not seem to help. He told me that he had had no good experiences recently. He didn't even seem interested in pursuing my question. I hadn't thought it was going to be this difficult.

Then I remembered the look of excitement I had seen on Gary's face as he followed me on his motorcycle to the pub. So I asked him if he enjoyed riding his bike. He said that didn't count. I wasn't about to let this one get away, so I asked him to tell me specifically what it felt like, sounded like, and looked like when he was enjoying a bike ride. With a little more coaching he began to open up and gave a powerful description of a favorite activity. It was comparatively brief, but it did contain a few key gestures and phrases.

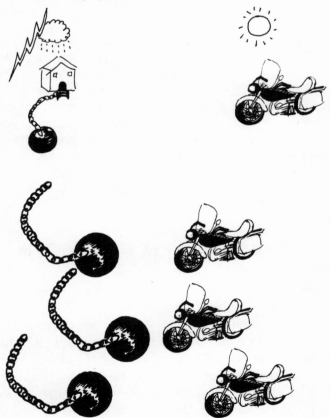

The third and final part of the exercise was a disaster. I couldn't maintain rapport for any more than 20 or 30 seconds. And Gary was very resistant to even entertaining the possibility that a pleasant, much less an exciting, experience could show up for him at home. I kept trying until it was obvious that he wasn't taking me seriously any more. At this point, I got frustrated and gave up on the whole idea of the exercise turning out successfully.

"IT" WORKED

in a different way.

Energy and enthusiam at home

The next day at work Gary approached me excitedly and told me that "it" had worked. At home the night before, he had found himself going about his regular evening routine with all sorts of energy and enthusiasm. A friend of his came over, and they began working on a design project that held his interest for hours. He thanked me for spending the time with him the previous evening and asked how the exercise worked. All I could say was, "I don't know!"

I learned a lot from this particular experience about persistently staying with neurolinguistic techniques. I also learned to entertain the possibility of obtaining favorable results outside the scope of my expectations.

Paul's sensory awareness was not fine-tuned enough to notice that the Scramble was working. Gary's verbal resistance blinded Paul to the efficacy of the positive impact of the motorcycle memory. Although we do seem to respond more intensely to negative experiences, these can be mitigated and even neutralized by enough positive associations. Paul was succeeding in the Scramble, even as he quit in frustration.

QUICKSKILL 3: HOW TO QUICKLY IMPROVE YOUR RESPONSE IN A CRUNCH

I define a "crunch" as any situation in which you are not getting what you want, in which you are outnumbered, outmaneuvered, and outtalked.

A crunch is when your client says, "There's no money budgeted for this." A crunch is when your boss says as you are leaving the office for a baseball game, "I need you to stay and work on this report tonight." A crunch is when your publisher says you need to write two more chapters.

When things are not going the way you want, when voices are rising and irritation is sneaking into the interaction, you need to

- Stop what you are doing
- Do something else

What else, specifically, should you do? Try moving your body into a completely different position. If at all feasible, get your communication partner to move as well.

Our thought processes and our body positions are linked so tightly that by changing position we can move our thinking toward new possibilities—new options. So if you are sitting down, stand up. If you are standing up, walk. Will this appear strange, perhaps inexplicable, to the other person? Not if you are congruent. You can reach for your briefcase or your purse and pull out a brochure, a list of figures, a laundry receipt. If you pull out a brochure or a list of figures, you may be able to use them to invite the other person to move in order to see them.

If you are not sure what might emerge from your briefcase, you may choose to stand up and walk around. Pacing is one type of movement that is often acceptable in a business office, and when you pace, the other person will have to shift somewhat to follow you. Moving physically when stuck mentally may be

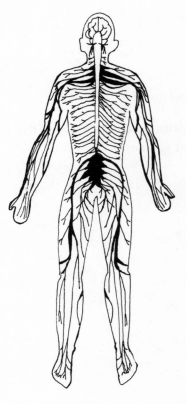

The spinal nerves could be viewed as extensions of the brain leading to all parts of the body.

new behavior for you, and it may seem strange at first, so practice it a few times before using it in an important transaction. For instance, try it when you and your child are locked in adversarial positions over a minor issue. Notice what happens. Moving may not create a thunderbolt, but it will change your thinking. As you change your thinking, new behaviors follow.

Is any of this manipulative? Only if you do not care about the other person's outcome. Moving yourself and the other person into the optimum physical and emotional state to obtain your outcomes is influencing—not manipulating. Orchestrating the physical moves necessary to do this is no more "manipulation" than choosing the right words to present your idea so that it is interesting to the other person. In fact, doing something else will result in your having more flexibility and perhaps more creative ways to look at situations.

In this chapter you learned three quickskills:

1. How to turn down your negative internal tapes

2. How to scramble communication to increase your energy level

Te—from a manuscript written in the sixth century B.C.—is the potential of being in the right place at the right time in the right frame of mind.

3. How to improve your response by moving when you find yourself in a crunch

Fine-tuning your brain for "the right frame of mind" is the subject of this book. The right place and time occur in rhythms, as you may begin to notice.

In Chapter 4 you will learn more about negative communication patterns and antidotes to them. But first, let's look more closely at the process of dovetailing, introduced in Chapter 1. Dovetailing is a vital step in successful communication.

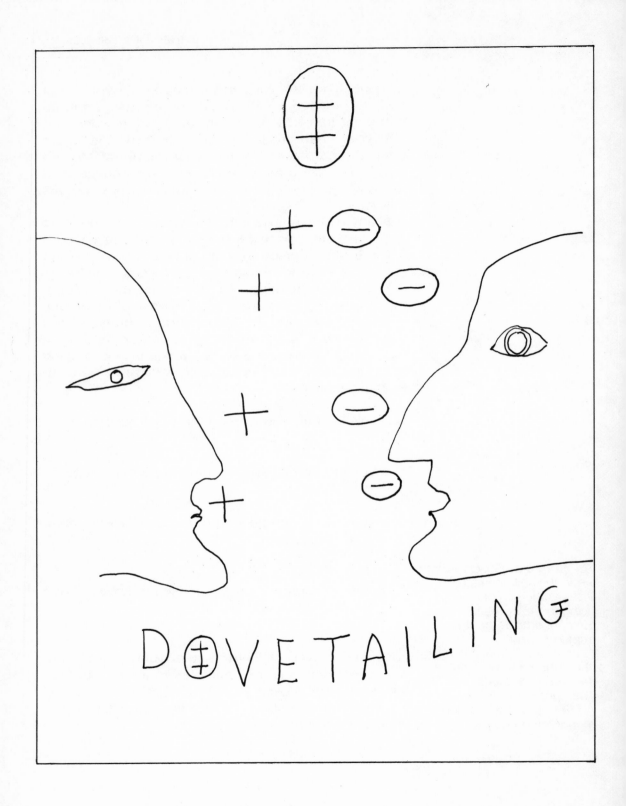

3
Dovetailing

When I am asked the most important concept to remember from our seminars in communication and negotiation, I answer, "Dovetailing." The seminar participants generally look a little puzzled at this response because many of the concepts taught in the seminars are more erudite, more sophisticated, more complex, and more difficult to remember. Dovetailing is so simple that it is hard to believe it has such impact. This one concept can dramatically raise your success rate if you take the time and energy to practice it.

"Dovetailing" is a woodworking term to describe the skillful fitting of two interlocking parts to form a strong joint or whole. When you and your communication partner dovetail, you will have a strong union based on mutually beneficial outcomes.

When dovetailing, be sure to express your outcome and the other person's outcome in sensory terms. What will you see, hear, and feel when you have your outcome? Then ask your communication partner what s/he will see, hear, and feel after gaining his/her outcome.

MY OUTCOME
YOUR OUTCOME
OUR OUTCOMES

MYOUR OUTCOMES

THE DOVETAILING CIRCLE

To see how dovetailing works, try this exercise: First, select an experience, business or personal, that did not turn out as well as you would have liked—one in which you and your partner did not achieve your outcomes.

Using the circle on the next page, write down your outcome on line 1. Then write down the other person's outcome on line 2. Use your imagination if you are not sure what the other person's outcome was. Describe the two outcomes in sensory-based terms. Write what you would see if you obtained your outcome. What would you hear? What would you feel? Now write down what your partner would see, hear, and feel after getting his/her outcome. Use your imagination, your intuition, if you do not know exactly. When you have filled in the blanks, can you dovetail an outcome to satisfy both your needs? Be creative and flexible in your solutions.

This is an excellent exercise to do with another person, who can play your partner after you describe the details of your interaction. A partner can also help provide new insights and options. Some people discover during the exercise that they and their original partners had identical outcomes, but their communication was so poor they never realized it. Thus they were left frustrated, with an unresolved conflict.

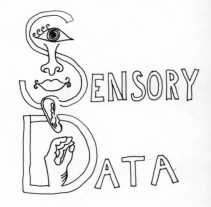

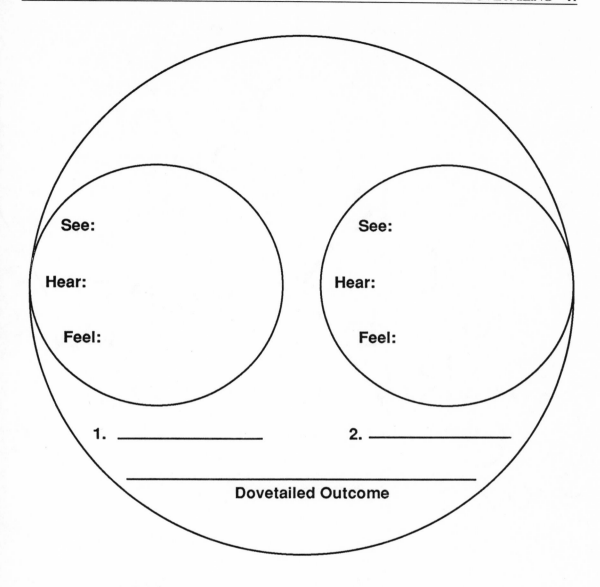

1. Write your outcome on line 1.
2. Write the other person's outcome on line 2.
3. In the small circles, write each of your outcomes in sensory-based terms. What would you and your partner *see, hear*, and *feel* if you had your outcomes?
4. Now, think of a creative way to obtain both outcomes.
5. Write this Dovetailed Outcome on the last line.

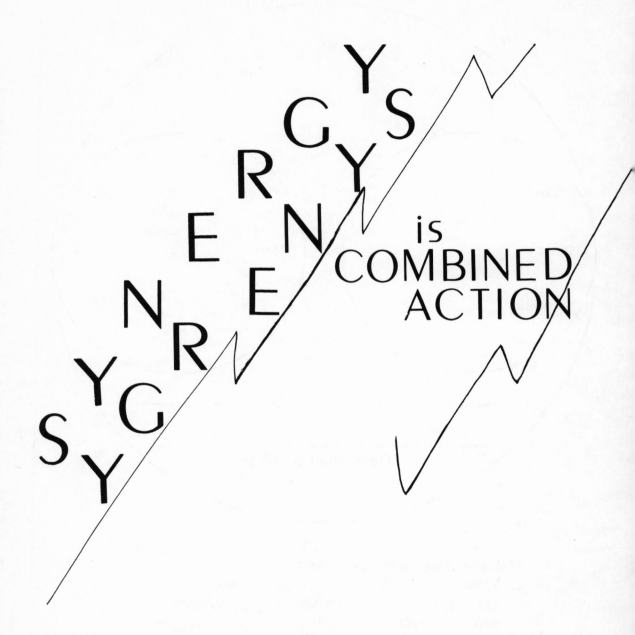

SYNERGY SYNERGY SYNERGY is COMBINED ACTION

WHEN YOU FORGET TO DOVETAIL

A vice president of one of the largest insurance companies in the world sat, nervously shifting in his chair, as he told about alienating a senior vice president five years before. His face was in shadow because of the light from the tall windows behind him. The light was glaring, but my eyes were slowly adjusting. His strained expression became clearer. Outside the tall windows were blue skies and Manhattan. Inside the room tension and anxiety seemed to mount as he concluded his story.

"I was trying to tell the guy that I would support him if he would change this one thing he was doing. But he never heard me." His dark blue suit reflected its expensive price tag, but as he talked, the suit somehow acquired a disheveled look.

"What's happening in your relationship now?" I settled back in my maroon, upholstered chair. I had heard this story in various forms many times.

"We're still cool and distant after five years. It's not good for my career to have that kind of response from someone one level up, even though I don't work for him directly."

"Do you understand what happened when you went in to talk to him?"

"No. I was just trying to get him to change one procedure. I wasn't going to blow the whistle on him, though I did have him—dead to rights."

Flexibility is being able to do something else when what you are doing is not working.

"What would have been in it for him? If he changed his procedures, how would the change have benefited him?"

"His entire department would have run more smoothly—fewer complaints, fewer time-consuming problems."

"Did he see that?"

Being right does not mean you will win.

"I guess not. He'd always done it his way, and he would not even consider the obviously better set of procedures."

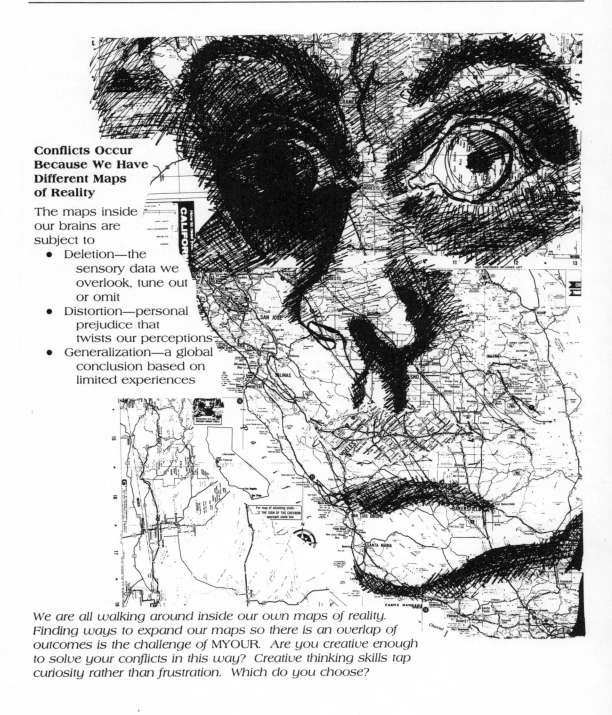

Conflicts Occur Because We Have Different Maps of Reality

The maps inside our brains are subject to

- Deletion—the sensory data we overlook, tune out or omit
- Distortion—personal prejudice that twists our perceptions
- Generalization—a global conclusion based on limited experiences

We are all walking around inside our own maps of reality. Finding ways to expand our maps so there is an overlap of outcomes is the challenge of MYOUR. Are you creative enough to solve your conflicts in this way? Creative thinking skills tap curiosity rather than frustration. Which do you choose?

"What did you want?"

"I wanted his division to run smoothly. That was my job—to examine procedures, results, and make recommendations."

"So you were just trying to do your job?"

"Well, yes, and my job then entailed dealing with all the problems his procedures were creating."

His body slumped lower in the chair, and his expression tightened as he remembered. His tie seemed to have slipped sideways. He managed to look frantic and defeated at the same time.

"So you had a personal outcome as well? Fewer hassles?"

"Yes."

"Can you think of how you could have presented him with a way to gain something for himself by implementing your procedures?"

"Well, it was obvious that his entire division would have benefited."

"It wasn't obvious to him."

"You're right. If it had been obvious, he would have done it." Long pause. "I never thought to make it clear how the procedure would help him personally."

"You were just a young whippersnapper with a lot of nuisance M.B.A. ideas that hadn't been tried in the real world, and you were trying to tell him how to do his job."

"I never looked at it from his viewpoint. I could have saved five years of worry about having created an enemy."

"Maybe."

"So what will you do with this idea, now?"

"Well, I'll think 'what's in it for the other guy?' before I move. And I'll spend some time with that senior vice president at our next division meeting practicing rapport techniques. He's not a bad guy—he just thinks he's right. He may be ready to bury the hatchet as well."

MYOUR may require some mental exercises to discover. So enjoy the challenge.

Filling Your Gum Ball Machine: First Step Toward Dovetailing

People are like empty gum ball machines that need to be filled by (1) finding out who they are, (2) having impact, and (3) connecting with another person, idea, or group. Once these three types of gum balls (identity, potency, and connectedness) have been collected to a satisfying level, then we can respond to the needs of others. When our gum ball machine is not filled with all three types, or colors, our behaviors reflect the deficit. It may be that we cannot respond to the psychological needs of others until our own are filled; no matter how many nickels people put in, we have no gum balls for them. Once we have collected a satisfactory level of gum balls, we respond to others' needs whether they have a nickel or not. We have learned how to fill our needs and can help them do the same.

Psychological Needs and Dovetailing

A sophisticated way to find creative solutions for conflict situations—so that you can dovetail—is to guess what the other person's most important psychological need is. If your guess is right—and you have a 33% chance that it is—you can tailor your proposal to satisfy this need. Needs of identity, potency, and connectedness seem to drive us all. When we have an unfulfilled need, our behaviors will push us to satisfy that need. The proposal that satisfies our top priority need will get our serious consideration. In business, the deficit need is often potency.

Many conflicts I have helped resolve were eliminated when the person in need was given power or status. I remember one situation when two people wanted one position, which had to be filled. There was serious competition for a few weeks, then my client sat down and discussed the situation with his competitor. The result was that my client got the duties of the position and the other person got the title. The other person needed a power position. My client did not give a hoot about the power; he wanted the challenge of the tasks involved.

During this last exchange his body had straightened somewhat, his face had relaxed, and his voice had become more assured. When he left, he was walking with energy.

If you forget everything else you've read in this book and remember to use

MYOUR

you will find yourself moving with the exceptional energy created when synergy is present. When individuals begin working as a team, when alignment is occurring, the results are beyond what most of us expect.

ANSWERS TO QUESTIONS

At seminars, people usually ask several questions about dovetailing. You may have questions similar to these:

- Why not call this win/win? Why introduce a new term?
- Will the other person tell me what s/he really wants?
- Will the other's outcome be company-oriented or personal?
- What if the other person keeps bringing in irrelevant information—outside our stated outcomes?
- What if we get bogged down and do not seem to be moving?
- How will I know we have completed dovetailing?
- What if I try all the approaches I know, and we still cannot dovetail?
- If the other person wants to take advantage of you and you are committed to dovetailing, does this put you at a disadvantage?

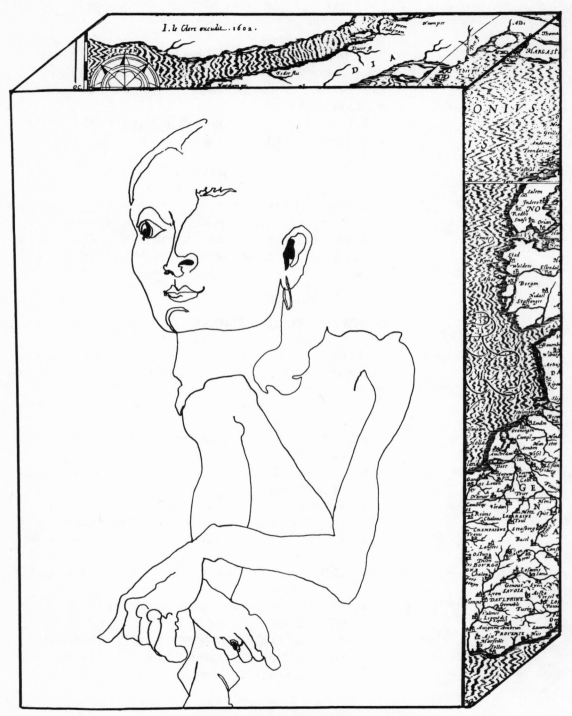

Maps of reality put us in boxes.

Let's look at these questions one at a time.

Why not call this win/win? Why introduce a new term? Dovetailing encompasses more than the usual win/win, which sometimes means compromise— when nobody gets what they really want. Dovetailing is when all parties are satisfied that the best deal possible has been made. I chose the word "dovetail" to remind you of the strong union that results when you both achieve your outcomes after using your thinking skills and joining with your communication partner to work out a satisfactory agreement. Saying that you want a win/win solution is not as good as behaving in creative ways to produce a mutual outcome that satisfies both parties.

This book offers many new skills, and if you use them along with your intuitive skills to create win/win+ solutions, then you are dovetailing.

Will the other person tell me what s/he really wants? Your communication partner will tell you what s/he wants if you have rapport. I define "rapport" in business as trust in competence for the task at hand. If you are having difficulty eliciting another's outcome, check rapport. Have you established your credibility? Do you trust that person's competence? If the answer to both these questions is "yes," then say something like, "We've been here for some time. I'm sure you have a goal in mind for this meeting. What would you like to accomplish in the next 10 minutes?"

If you still do not get an answer, then ask a question. "If it were 10 minutes from now, and you felt sure this interview had been successful, what would you see?" Pause. If no answer, "What would you hear that would let you know we had accomplished your outcome for this meeting?" Long pause. If you have rapport and still do not elicit a response, do something different. Take your client for a walk, for

Opposite:

Our maps of reality put us in boxes so that we cannot see new options to our conflicts, cannot hear new solutions, and cannot get a feeling for what it is like to let go of old, worn-out beliefs that are no longer working toward our outcomes. A belief that most conflicts can be resolved by dovetailing creates new awareness of possible options.

coffee, for lunch. If this does not work, you might want to reevaluate your outcome. Your time is valuable too.

Will the other's outcome be company-oriented or personal? Most business people will have an outcome that is both business and personal in nature. You do best to *pretend* this outcome is strictly for the good of the business. However, we all are interested in doing good things for ourselves, as well as our corporation, institution, or company. This self-interest is natural, normal, and practiced. Accept this personal/business interlacing. Your business expects you to have dual outcomes—yours and the corporation's. So count on your partner's having both a personal and a business outcome, and be creative in offering a product, service, or idea that satisfies both.

I saw a news interview of a man who had been terminated after 18 years with the same company. The interview was at the end of his last day on the job.
Interviewer: "Do you have a new job?"
Worker: "No."
Interviewer: "Have you looked for a new job?"
Worker: "Not really."
Interviewer: "When were you informed of the termination?"
Worker: "Six months ago. They said I was to spend the six months looking for a job."
Interviewer: "So what have you been doing for the last six months?"
Worker (pride in voice): "I've gone to work every day."
Interviewer: "Even though you were told to spend the time finding a new job?"
Worker: "Well, yes. I really liked my regular job."
Interviewer: "What will you do now?
Worker: "I don't know."

LOYALTY

Do not confuse loyalty with stupidity.

"When people work to their full capacity, when they feel in sync with their cowork-ers, when everything comes together on cue although completely unplanned, align-ment is present."

—Reinventing the
Corporation

What if the other person keeps bringing in irrele-vant information—outside our stated outcomes? Lis-ten to the irrelevancies as long as you comfortably can. Your partner may be using small talk to cover up a decision-making process. S/he may need time to think and may not feel comfortable just remaining silent. If your partner does fall into silence, remind yourself that s/he may be making a decision, and keep quiet. I have heard sales representatives tell about listening to war stories or metaphors with no point for months before making a sale. You must decide whether listening out the irrelevancies is going to be worthwhile.

A pattern-interrupt, described in Chapter 4, may work to stop the irrelevancies, war stories, whatever. But pattern-interrupts are risky, so be careful. There are many elements to a successful interaction. What works in one instance may not work in another. What works usually fits neatly into one of these cat-egories: (1) my outcome, (2) your outcome, and (3) dovetailing.

Alignment and dovetailing are similiar magical proc-esses. "Magical" means we do not completely under-stand how they occur.

One strategy for clients who stray off the subject is to begin the interaction, "I know you're busy, and I have another meeting this morning, too. I think we can accomplish what we need to do in an hour. Do you agree?"

Dovetailing the outcomes of each member of a group is essential for synergy. Dovetailing can be done covertly or overtly, whichever is appropriate.

Strategy for people who conceal their outcome

(*usually from fear of not getting it if anybody knows*). If someone does not know what s/he wants, have that person move forward in time—act *as if* it is 15 minutes or 5 years in the future and see what is happening, hear what is going on, and get a feeling for having achieved whatever s/he wants. Acting *as if* can be a quickskill all by itself.

For instance, you might say:
   "When you agreed to meet with me, you must have had something in mind. If the next 15 minutes are useful for you—if you could get what you want during them— what would that be?"

You will probably be able to design other creative strategies appropriate for your clients in specific situations.

What if we get bogged down and do not seem to be moving? If you get sidetracked from obtaining your outcome or from eliciting your communication partner's outcome, your next best move is to move— shift in your chair or, if you are standing, take a few steps. Then say, "Lets go over what we've agreed upon so far and decide on an appropriate next step." Maybe you will need other words than these; however, the process is *summarize, and specify next step,* from the meeting format PEGASUS (Chapter 1). If you can proceed to the next step now, fine! If not, at least you are moving—maybe out the door, but that has some compensations.

How will I know when we have completed dove-tailing? When both of you have gained your outcomes.

or
"What would you see that would convince you the next 15 minutes were successful?"

or
"What would you hear during the next 15 minutes that would be useful?"

or
"What do we need to accomplish during this meeting in order for you to feel good about this use of your time?"

What if I try all the approaches I know, and we still cannot dovetail? Congratulate yourself on your flexibility, then applaud yourself for having so many resources, then celebrate the fact that you know there is no point in spending more time on this project. Shake your adversary's hand and move on. Once outside the office, shake your arms and shake your head and let go of resentment for the time you spent. One of my friends used to say, "Some things never were, and some were never meant to be."

If the other person wants to take advantage of you and you are committed to dovetailing, does this put you at a disadvantage? Actually, the easiest people in the world to defeat are those who are up to no good. If the other person is determined *not* to dovetail, then s/he is certainly not going to be able to manipulate you. Once you recognize a win/lose game, the biggest problem is not to laugh at it. People who are stuck in win/lose are so transparent in their behaviors, and yet usually so obtuse in their sensory acuity, that you need to be kind to them. They lead miserable existences, many of them, and constantly cause themselves trouble. Be kind and disengage.

Dovetailing Occurs in a Conflict When Maps of Reality Match or Overlap

All our maps are different in some ways and similar in some ways. Communication can uncover areas where our maps overlap. By adding new points of view to our maps, we can expand our understanding of others' viewpoints so that overlaps occur.

Each of us comes to a conflict situation with vastly different maps. By communicating our intentions and learning the intentions of the other parties, we can begin to find areas of agreement, of overlap. These small areas of agreement can be expanded by adding new insights about the others' outcomes, our own outcomes, and what additional options are possible.

DOVETAILING CLOSES A SALE

One of my former students, let's call him George, is the sales manager of a CT equipment company. CT scanners sell for about $1 million, and in the last few years competition has been fierce. As sales manager, George is called in when one of his salespeople has a good prospect who will not close.

Recently, George spent an hour with a certain prospect, who represented a large hospital that did not own a CT scanner. At the end of an hour, he realized he was doing no better than his salesman had. The prospect was courteous but was not buying. George took a deep breath and, as he told me later, asked himself this question, "What would Genie do now?" The answer came quickly, "Dovetail."

"I felt embarrassed," he said. He had been in sales 15 years and should have been able to figure it out himself. Thinking "dovetail," he realized he did not have enough information about this prospect's outcome. He knew his own outcome, he knew the outcomes of other prospects who had become buyers, but he did not know *exactly* what this customer wanted the CT scanner to do for the hospital and for him personally.

The prospective buyer had earlier complained about the number of other hospitals in the same area and the intense competition for patients. George took a deep breath, sat back, and asked him, "Would you tell me a little more about your competition and what your strategy is to position yourself as a leader?"

One hour later George had made a $1 million sale, and he phoned to tell me of the role dovetailing had played.

Try dovetailing; it works.

Successful Communication

Before You begin—   Know what You want

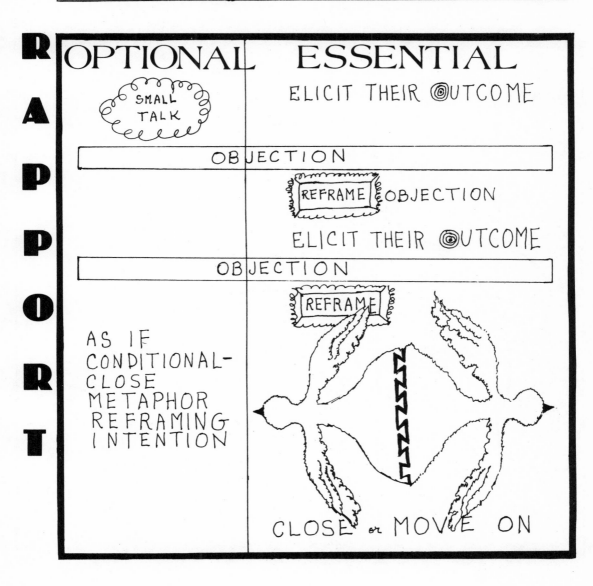

RAPPORT

OPTIONAL	ESSENTIAL
SMALL TALK	ELICIT THEIR OUTCOME

OBJECTION

REFRAME OBJECTION

ELICIT THEIR OUTCOME

OBJECTION

REFRAME

AS IF
CONDITIONAL-
CLOSE
METAPHOR
REFRAMING
INTENTION

CLOSE or MOVE ON

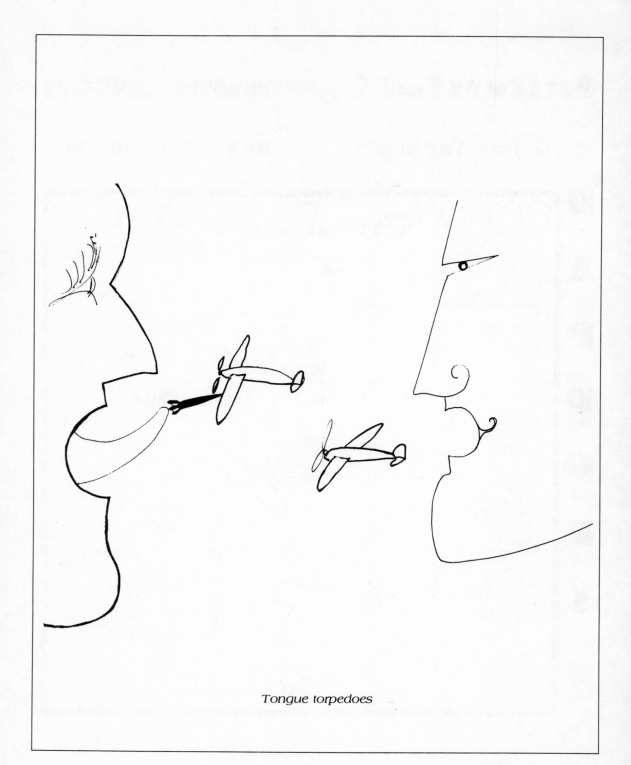

Tongue torpedoes

4
Negative Communication Patterns

Positive communication is an interaction that leaves all participants energized, feeling respected for their contributions and viewpoints, and looking forward with curiosity and confidence to the next encounter. Creative problem-solving flourishes in a positive communication setting.

Negative communication, on the other hand, often drains the energy of the participants, leaving them feeling inadequate for having a difference of opinion. They may dread upcoming meetings and be reluctant to give input for fear of being "wrong." They may choose silence in order to avoid the feelings of diminished confidence and self-worth that they have experienced in the past. Creative problem-solving is stillborn in a negative communication setting.

ANYONE CAN PLAY ONE UP ONE DOWN

You are a manager.
I am only an employee.
You are a vice president.
I am only a manager.
You are the president.
I am only a vice president.
You are the chairman.
I am only the president.
You are a man.
I am only a woman.
You are a woman.
I am only a man.
You are a professor.
I am only a student.
You are a junior.
I'm only a sophomore.
You're five.
I'm four.

WHY WOULD ANYONE WANT TO?

At some time or other we have all been involved in an unsuccessful communication. When it was over, we felt frustrated, fatigued, and often guilty. Such reactions are frequently the result of these negative communication patterns: one up, one down, blaming, complaining, guilt, and apologizing. Let's look at each of these patterns and some specific antidotes.

ONE UP

One up is that mental state in which you act as if you are better, smarter, or more successful than your communication partner. You may not regularly operate in this state, but you have encountered it in others. Here are some of the ways one-upsmanship is played in business:

- Saying "Continue talking; I'm listening" while opening and reading mail, answering the phone, correcting the daily schedule
- Leaning on a seated subordinate's shoulder while giving instructions
- Looking at the ceiling when a subordinate makes a suggestion
- Not returning phone calls from salespeople, vendors, or those lower on the corporate ladder
- Always being "in a meeting" to those same groups of human beings
- Saying "I'll get back to you" and not bothering to do so
- Shifting voice tone toward condescension when another reveals his/her lower status in the organization
- Mumbling "That's interesting" to any suggestion a subordinate makes and dismissing the idea at once

- Shaking a finger in someone else's face
- Ignoring a passing greeting in the elevator or hall
- Mixing up subordinates' names even after months in the same office
- Placing both feet on the desk so the other person must peer around them
- Looking out the window during an entire interaction—never once facing the presenter

ONE DOWN

One down is that mental state in which you act as if you are less smart, less talented, or less successful than your communication partner.

The one down attitude works occasionally. Some people in power positions demand this attitude before they will permit rapport. And, in fact, this is a fun game to play as long as you know it is a weird game and you can quit any time you want. The problem is that, in business, people sometimes get caught in this attitude and cannot change it. They even begin to believe it. The one down attitude may become unconscious—out of conscious control. It is terrible to feel one down most of the time.

Usually, successful people want to interact with colleagues, not one downers, because they know instinctively that one-on-one works better. The one downer is resentful and secretly wishes the one up would fail. One up, one down attitudes do not produce successful interactions.

If you take one-upsmanship maneuvers personally, it is no wonder you may begin to feel one down. Such behaviors should be noted and categorized (boorish, impolite, dumb, or whatever pejorative word comes to mind). You should decide whether you need to work with this person and quickly generate a positive internal state so you can succeed in this milieu.

Check your chenille.

Up the Down Internal State

There is an antidote to both the up and the down mental state. Recognize that each of us is good at some things, expert at some, and lousy at some. Most of us have areas in which we excel. There are probably people more skillful than we at most things; however, we each have something to offer our employees, our managers, and our company. As long as we are happy with our behavior and like ourselves, we need never be one down. Find one special thing—or even better, several things—you like about yourself and go one-on-one with everyone.

One down can be a game you play out of choice for a particular outcome that is important enough for you to be a floormat. If people are walking over you a lot, however, check your chenille. Floormats invite walkovers.

The one up attitude (often seen in headwaiters) is usually a loser too. If you spend a lot of time trying to convince yourself that you are better than everyone else or that you are no worse than anyone else, try this. Move this attitude from the unconscious to the conscious level. For one week, ask yourself, "How am I better than X?" Then consciously pay attention to how much more skillful, beautiful, intelligent, rich, nice, tasteful, you are than each person you talk with.

As soon as you have answered how much better you are, ask yourself two other questions: "In what areas is s/he more skillful than I am?" "What does s/he know that I do not know?" You can grow out of limited thinking patterns quickly by using these three questions. These questions and answers work for balancing both one up and one down states.

One-upsmanship is an attitude that will not lead to success—unless you want to be a headwaiter in a restaurant that goes out of business every few months.

As for one-downsmanship, if you believe you are really and truly one down, when you interact with someone who prefers to deal with equals, you will fail and may never know why. Your mental, physical, and financial health will improve as you erase one-downsmanship.

BLAMING

- "Your division's profits are down."
- "You missed the deadline."
- "Your report is confusing."
- "Your analysis misses the point."
- "You did not make your quota."

Can you find the other message in these negative sentences? When the boss tells you "Your division's profits are down," s/he is often implying "and it's your fault" rather than "and how can we change this?"

When the boss says, "You missed the deadline," what s/he means is, "How could you be so incompetent?" Your boss is usually not thinking of how to lighten your work load so you can meet the deadline.

When the boss says, "Your report is confusing," the message really is "and so is your thinking." S/he is not offering to help you organize your report. S/he is blaming you.

Blaming is so prevalent when hierarchies are part of the establishment that subordinates become accustomed to being blamed—even for events over which they have no control. And blaming others is comforting; then we are off the hook. Sometimes we are even one up. Some managers have to find something wrong with everything.

The problem with affixing blame, even if you affix it correctly, is that the situation is not changed. The same energy spent in finding the person to blame could be used more wisely—to change the situation for the better. Instead of an accusing statement like, "You missed the deadline," a more productive communication might be "How could you and I, working together, get those financial reports to the vice president by the first of each month?" In the second statement, you are moving toward a solution.

Earlier I said that in affixing blame the situation had not changed. This is not quite true. Actually, you are losing ground because the employee blamed how

Antidotes to Blaming

- Look for a solution.
- Make the implicit explicit: "Are you blaming me?"

feels guilty, and this guilt is counterproductive to finding a solution to the problem. The employee is now occupied with guilt and ways to protect his/her position, often to such an extent that thinking about solutions is curtailed.

Many bosses spend so much time trying to place blame and many employees spend so much time trying to protect themselves from blame (by writing memos, cataloging minor work activities, typing instructions, etc.) that very little in the way of positive work gets done. Work time is consumed by attacks and defenses against attacks.

When you give up blaming and problem-solve instead, you move from unsuccessful interactions to successful ones. If your boss asks, "Will that report be finished on time?" you might respond, "I can complete the report on time if I put aside X and Y. Shall I do that?" Instead of blaming—a lack of time or too many projects—you offer a solution. Now the ball is in your boss's court.

COMPLAINING

- "The copy machine is smudging the letters."
- "Nobody notified me of the meeting."
- "Someone messed up the files."
- "Traffic is so bad. It took an hour to get to work."
- "We don't have enough staff."

Although these statements may be factual, the tone with which they are delivered often makes them complaining statements.

Complaining and blaming are closely related, but there are differences. Blame is more direct, even when implied. Blame is a cannonball; complaints are scattershot. You feel the hit, but not as strongly. Complaining has strong hints of blame, but the guilt does not all go to the recipient—only most of it. Many people feel almost as guilty in response to complaints as in response to blame.

Besides the guilt elicited in the receiver, complaining has another negative effect: It reminds the other person of all the things in his/her life that are not right. Complaining directs attention to what is wrong. As long as you are noticing what is wrong, you will not notice what is right.

We all perform better when we feel good about our abilities. When we feel competent, confident, and creative, we produce extraordinary accomplishments. "Your desk is a shambles" is not likely to lead to an extraordinary performance on the part of your subordinate.

"Your desk is a shambles"

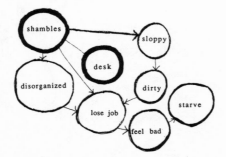

The associations are not likely to be

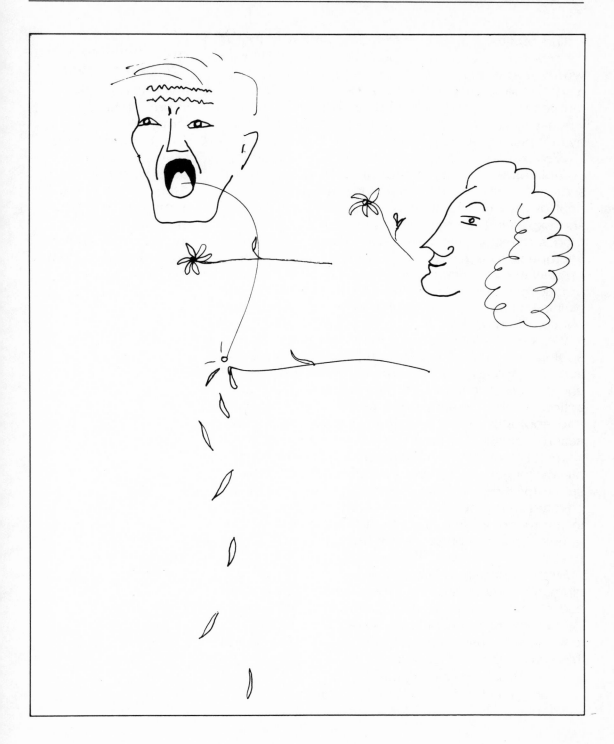

The biggest problem with complaining is that it cancels out the potential of positive communication—words that energize your colleagues and subordinates. Guilt and complaining seldom energize communication. You are hoisted on your own petard when you hamper your subordinates' performances by complaining and blaming.

I realized quite suddenly one day that blaming, complaining, and explaining or apologizing (in the sense of justifying my own actions) made up a great deal of my communication. Blaming, complaining, and explaining are seductive to me; however, these modes of expression were quite useless when I was attempting to achieve goals in the business world. Up until that moment of realization, I was an expert in producing subtle guilt in others by blaming and complaining, charmingly, of course, so my hearers would not complain back.

We are all so used to blaming, complaining and apologizing that we hardly notice such communication. However, negative communication reduces the energy, the aliveness, of the participants in the interaction. When I realized that complaining, blaming, and apologizing were all impediments to positive action, I decided to stop using words for such messages. It took strong resolution to follow through. I bit my tongue throughout the first day, and I hardly spoke for three weeks while I broke the habit. I discovered that practically every conversational gambit in my repertoire fell into one of these negative categories. I went through a lot of frustration while trying to quit.

Simultaneously, I noticed a lot of other people blaming, complaining, and explaining. No wonder I had not noticed before that I had been communicating negatively and habitually. Most of the people I listened to were using negative terms, too. Do you find this hard to believe? Listen:

- "You like crisis management."
- "You don't know how to delegate."

An Antidote to Any Negative Pattern

If you find yourself in one of these patterns, take a deep breath, move your body into some other position, and ask yourself, "What is my outcome here and now?" Notice the difference in the communication from that point on.

Guilt is an energy drain.

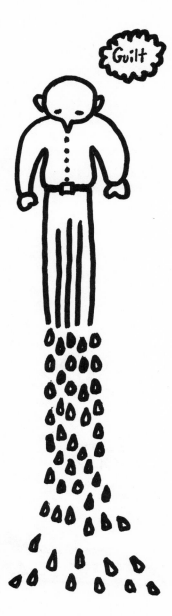

- "You talk too fast" or ". . . too slow."
- "Your handwriting is unintelligible."
- "We need more time to work on this project."
- "They don't make things the way they used to."
- "The work ethic is dead."
- "Old age is difficult."
- "Being young is hard."

Do these comments sound familiar? They ought to; they make up a large proportion of everyday conversation for most people.

You can determine whether a complainer has found someone or something to blame by paying attention to voice tone. A really good complainer can always attach a little blame to the listener simply by tone of voice.

- "The U.S. automobile industry is in trouble." (Implied: "You drive a foreign car. You are adding to the problem.")
- "It's raining again." (Implied: "It's your fault.")
- "Everything is so expensive." (Implied: "You don't make enough money.")

The more subtle this tone is in blaming, the greater the guilt the listener feels. Subtle messages often slip by the conscious mind and drip their guilt into the unconscious.

Antidote to Complaining

You can make the implicit blaming aspect of complaining explicit. Your partner is probably unaware of blaming you for the economic downturn in the U.S. automobile industry because you drive a foreign car. Your explicit statement can be light, like a joke: "Well, I won't take credit for Detroit's predicament. Say, though, have you seen next year's models? They've got some great new designs." You have now shifted from a negative energy drain to a positive, forward-looking mode.

GUILT

Blaming and complaining often produce guilt in listeners. However, there are other times we feel guilty about doing or not doing something that a part of us wanted to do. In other words, we have an internal conflict.

When you feel guilty, when you have an internal conflict, your communication will often produce erratic responses from others. Because of your internal conflict, you are sending double messages, and so you are not congruent in your communication. (In Chapter 6, we will look at the importance of congruent communication and ways to achieve it.) Whether you are talking with your boss, your secretary, or your peers, if you feel guilty about what you are communicating, you will not have the impact you want.

For example, if you realize you are feeling guilty about asking for a raise, for typing help after 5 p.m., or for assistance on a project, you can interrupt your communication, go off by yourself, sort out what is going on inside, and then reopen the communication later. A statement such as: "Excuse me, I forgot something I have to do now—I'll get back to you," is better than engaging in a guilt-laced interaction.

Guilt has two important functions. When others use it to get us to do what they want, it is a form of control. Guilt may also be used as punishment—usually punishment for not having done what other people wanted.

"Shoulds" and "should nots" usually indicate controls from others. Even wants and desires may be guilt provoking because we have ignored the controls of others in favor of our own desires. Many of us have been programmed to go straight from desire to guilt. Do not pass Go. Do not collect $200. Just collect guilt.

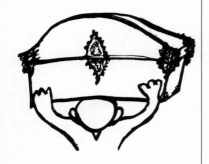

Antidote to Guilt

Feeling guilty is not useful. Learn to recognize guilt for what it is; then let it go. Turn down your audiotapes, shift your attention to some other internal feeling, or access your resource state (Chapter 9). It will seem strange at first—as if all your life you had been carrying a heavy steamer trunk on your back until someone suggested, "Why don't you put that thing down?"

Once you erase guilt as an internal state, you will find you are more congruent in communicating, and more successful.

You recognize positive and negative communication by the results.

APOLOGIZING

Earlier I mentioned apologizing and explaining as two communication patterns I learned to change. I think both of these are aligned with blaming and complaining. The time-wasting dynamics of blaming, complaining, and guilt are fairly clear, but how do apologizing and justifying impede productive action? Consider this collection of justifications/explanations, all wrapped up with an apology, like a bow:

"I'm sorry to be late with this report. Accounting didn't get the figures to me on time. Then we had a temporary typist who kept making mistakes. And, would you believe it, the copy machine was down all morning. I'm really sorry that you didn't have this for your meeting."

What a time waster! The fact is that you do what you do at any given moment because you think your behavior is the perfect solution, given what you know at the time. It is true that later you might learn or recall information to make you decide that your action was inappropriate. In that case, an apology may indeed be in order. So waste no time, apologize. Some people like to receive apologies when they think you have been out of line.

However, apologies are the cheapest coin in the realm. Apologies are only words. Words are easily produced and fade fast. Instead of "being sorry" for what you did, you might consider doing something else—volunteer to take over an assignment, for example.

Behavior is high-quality information. If you decide your previous behavior was truly inappropriate, send flowers instead of apologies, and get on with your productive work. If you cannot afford flowers, write a positive note telling the other person something you like about him/her.

If complaining, blaming, and apologizing are the staples you rely on in daily conversation, you may be wondering what you will talk about if you decide to give them up. After about two weeks you will probably think of something, or you may choose to remain silent. Being with someone and not talking can be great. Try it.

Once you have begun to appreciate the power that words carry, you will probably choose to use them less, especially in business. If your words are not moving your communication partners toward your group outcome, then do not utter them. Successful business people use words to establish rapport, to exchange information, to brainstorm, to problem-solve, and to summarize agreements and decisions. If your words are being used for these reasons, great. If not, be silent, and use your thinking processes to help you obtain your outcome.

Antidote to Negative Behavior

1. Notice behavior.
2. Categorize behavior:
    one up
    one down
    blaming
    complaining
    guilt
    apologizing
3. That's his/her behavior. I can respond in whatever way I wish. I can indulge that attitude. I can exaggerate my response (somewhat dangerous).
4. Shall I stay? Shall I leave?
5. What behavior can I adopt to change his/her behavior?

In this chapter were presented clues to help you recognize negative communication early enough to use an antidote— early enough so that you still have some energy left.

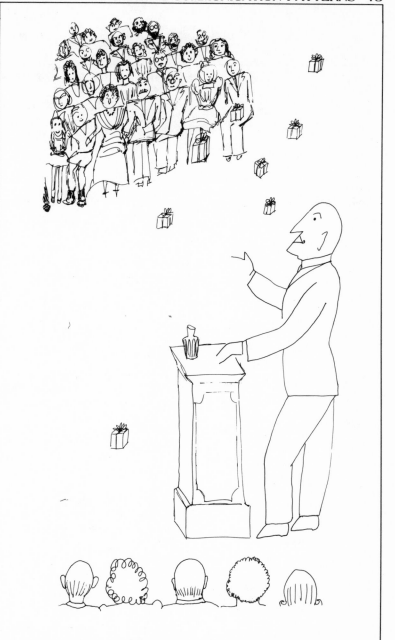

Some "positive" communication goes unrecognized because of boredom, misunderstanding, or presuppositions. You get to decide whether communication is positive or negative for you.

Antidotes to Negative

Patterns	Specific Antidotes to Negative Patterns in Self
One up	Ask yourself: "How is X better than I?"
One down	Ask yourself: "How am I better than X?" Access your resource state.
Blaming	Take responsibility for your life. Quit blaming luck, chance, others, or the institutions. Reframe. Access your resource state.
Complaining	Take responsibility for your life. List three positive things about yourself. Access your resource state.
Guilt	Recognize the feeling and take some positive action, or let the feeling go by replacing it with another. Access your resource state. Reframe.
Apologizing	Know that you are doing the best you can given your life experiences and the words you have used to describe them. Access your resource state. Chew saltwater taffy.

Note: Some of these antidotes, such as reframing and accessing a resource state, are explained in later chapters.

Communication Patterns

Patterns	Specific Antidotes to Negative Patterns in Others
One up	Access your resource state. Move. Pattern-interrupt. Ask yourself: "What is my outcome?" Remember a previous appointment (at the White House?).
One down	Make the implicit explicit: "Are you feeling one down?" Give a compliment.
Blaming	Ask for clarification: "Are you blaming me for the project failure?" Ask, "How can we solve this problem together?" Scramble. Reframe. Disconnect.
Complaining	Ask yourself: "Given all the possible things to talk about, how can s/he choose this negative experience? Maybe I could find questions that would elicit this information." Scramble. Pattern-interrupt. Reframe. Do business elsewhere.
Guilt	Categorize the behavior without verbalizing it: "S/he's feeling guilty." Then respond in a way to change the behavior of the other person. If the other person is feeling guilty, let him/her off the hook. Ask, in appropriate language, "Are you feeling uncomfortable? Would you like to talk about it?" Then suggest a positive action.
Apologizing	Recognize the pattern without verbalizing it: "S/he's apologizing for what s/he did." Tell the person you understand how s/he could have selected that behavior. Say, "There are no mistakes—just experiments that didn't work out. Let's move on."

PATTERN-INTERRUPT:
A POWERFUL INTERVENTION

If someone besieges you with negative communication that drains your energy, you may choose to *pattern-interrupt* that person. Interrupting another person's behavior pattern often has surprising results. A "behavior pattern" is a sequence of habitual responses that follow one another so quickly they seem to be one action. Any group of behaviors ordinarily used in sequence—in a known pattern—can be interrupted.

A behavior pattern

Some examples of pattern-interrupts are (1) offering a handshake, then quickly withdrawing your hand; (2) interrupting a story—your own or another's; and (3) halting abruptly while walking in rhythm with someone.

A pattern-interrupt

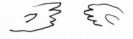

A sudden, unexpected movement on your part may also pattern-interrupt the other person. Sometimes pattern-interrupts break rapport, so they are to be used with caution.

Pattern-interrupts can cause responses that you should be aware of. The person whose pattern has been interrupted experiences momentary confusion, and in some cases, even amnesia. If the confusion is sufficiently uncomfortable, the person becomes susceptible to suggestion from anyone. In other words, the interrupted person wants to trade confusion for clarity and will go along with someone else's clarity for a short time.

Unscrupulous people may use this technique to manipulate others for a short while. Avoid pattern-interrupts unless you are sure any suggestion made is leading toward the other's outcome. As long as you are definitely dovetailing, a pattern-interrupt can speed up the process of changing negative communication to positive communication.

Pattern-Interrupt

Interrupting a pattern may cause this sequence of responses:
1. A feeling of confusion
2. Susceptibility to outside suggestion
3. Amnesia for the entire experience
4. Return to normal thinking patterns
5. Resentment if you have been taken advantage of

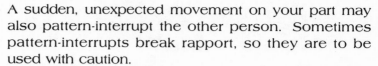

*Use pattern-interrupts with caution—
and only when dovetailing.*

Your job is to make sure that I don't look like a half-baked dimwit.

Now that we have explored some negative communication patterns, let's review the three steps to successful communication once again.

MY OUTCOME   1. Knowing what you want

YOUR OUTCOME   2. Finding out what the other person wants

OUR OUTCOMES   3. Dovetailing your outcomes for a win/win+ solution

At times indirect communication will achieve the results you want better than a direct, straightforward message will. Usually, straight talk works best in business situations; sometimes, however, you may need an indirect influencing tactic. A metaphor is one of the most useful, and fun, indirect methods of communication you can use. Chapter 5 plays with metaphors.

Skills that will turn unsuccessful interactions into successful ones:
- Change internal states quickly.
- Notice patterns of responses in others.
- Determine what these patterns of responses mean.
- Hear voice shifts that indicate a change of mind.
- Establish rapport.
- Regain rapport if lost.
- Create congruent patterns for your own presentations.
- Be flexible in your choice of language and in behaviors.
- Use comparisons and metaphors when straight talk is not working.
- Correct "stuck places," where your behavior is robotlike because of past experiences.

5
Communicating with Metaphors

Widespread culturally, metaphors are older than the written word. Shaped into parables, fables, and folktales, metaphors were used to teach, to offer insight, and to persuade. Basically, metaphors are comparisons, ranging from a simple comparison of two things to a series of comparisons, either stated or implied, inside a tale told with a purpose. In business, metaphors are useful when indirect communication is preferable to direct communication—for example, when you have to tell your boss that s/he is wrong.

Metaphors work on both our conscious and our unconscious minds. Our conscious mind responds to simple comparisons; our unconscious is intrigued by complex metaphors and searches out the purpose or meaning behind the elements in the tale. When you use complex metaphors, you can arrange the sequence to suit your own purpose and that of your partner in the communication process. Metaphors work best when the purposes—the outcomes—of all communicating parties dovetail.

When you use a complex metaphor, your purpose may seem well hidden, but the unconscious mind is very clever at finding the meaning. So your hearers will probably understand your meaning, at least unconsciously.

The unconscious mind has all five perceptual doors open all the time. This mind is not bound by sequential processing, and it seems to know more than the conscious mind. It is the unconscious that appreciates, is amused by, and learns from complex metaphors.

I want to make a point for skeptics: You can communicate with the unconscious mind—your own as well as that of others. Advertisers do this all the time. When you are directing an important communication to the unconscious mind, you would do well to line up the knowledge and energy of the conscious with the knowledge and energy of the unconscious mind. One way to accomplish this alignment is through metaphors.

Metaphors influence in a subtle way. A well-designed, complex metaphor is a communication that employs the unconscious at its most elegant and its most beautiful. A metaphor is the polite way to invite someone else to join you in dovetailing outcomes. And a little humor adds to a metaphor's effectiveness.

Fairy tales, folktales, and myths are usually metaphors that present potential points of view—other ways to look at events. The ugly duckling tale—in which the awkward cygnet develops into a graceful swan—is an intricate and lovely metaphor with several levels of meaning: (1) There is no ugliness, only difference. (2) There are others like you somewhere. (3) Even when things look bleak, do not despair; change is coming. (4) You are beautiful, and do not forget it, even if those around you do not recognize your beauty.

Our reality is a map of reality—not reality itself. A map of Texas is not Texas.

I do not recommend that you tell the ugly duckling story to your boss, even if your message is that s/he is strange but beautiful. Make up your own metaphor, and use a subject your boss finds engrossing, entertaining, and fascinating. The traditional metaphor can be very useful in business communication, especially if it is succinct. And, at times, a complex metaphor can be very successful in a business situation. Let's look more closely at three types of metaphors and their use in communication.

SIMPLE METAPHORS

The simple metaphor—the direct comparison—is useful in helping the conscious mind compare or relate a known object, person, or concept to an unfamiliar object, person, or concept. A simple metaphor can place something new and strange on your hearer's map of reality in a way that makes it understandable. This is a comfortable and natural way for the hearer to learn about the unknown. "Space shuttle" and "primordial soup" are simple metaphors.

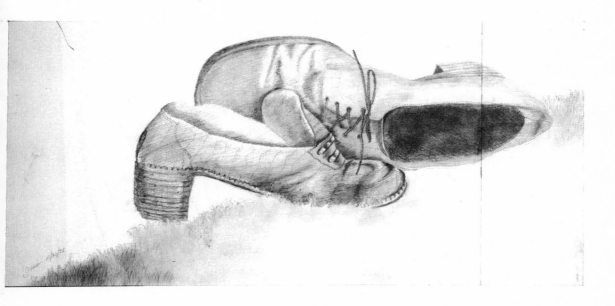

POINT-OF-VIEW METAPHORS

A comparison that contains a particular point of view seeks to change the way the listener looks at a situation already coded on his/her map of reality. Examples, from the folklore of the Deep South, where I grew up, include: "You're as slow as molasses," "She is cuter than a basketful of speckled pups," and "He runs around like a chicken with his head cut off."

Speakers and writers often use the point-of-view metaphor to highlight an unnoticed aspect of something familiar so the audience can see it with new eyes. The "new eyes," supplied by the writer or speaker, carry his/her viewpoint. At this level metaphor begins to influence as well as teach.

Here is a point-of-view metaphor used successfully by a senior vice president of a large international bank. After listening to his division's position on a bank problem, which was that the problem belonged not to that division but to operations, he went to the chalkboard and drew a ship's bow with some stick figures on it. He waited a minute; then he completed the drawing, showing the stern sinking. Then he said, "Your position on this matter reminds me of what those people on the bow are saying: 'I'm sure glad we're not at the other end of the boat.'"

Delivering such a metaphor might not be too difficult if you are the boss, and it does make the point. Metaphors like these have a succinct quality that makes them especially appropriate for business.

Metaphors are needed because we all have different maps of reality.

COMPLEX METAPHORS

This third-level metaphor is designed specifically to influence. Complex metaphors send information and guidance to your partner's unconscious. This type of metaphor involves an intricate organization of parallel elements.

The complex metaphor is the most sophisticated communication tool available for indirect messages. With complex metaphors, you can influence on an unconscious level. When you use such metaphors, you must be very careful to dovetail your outcomes and those of your partner. Otherwise your listener's unconscious will probably resist your influence. Conversely, if you do dovetail, you will be establishing an environment in which the other person's unconscious will work with you.

CREATING A COMPLEX METAPHOR

One way to make sure the other person will hear your metaphor is to dress your key points in a story about a subject that interests him/her. Tennis, golf, fishing, cooking, hunting, and pets are all subjects that lend themselves to metaphors. If your partner is interested in golf, do not use a fishing story. Use a golf story for your series of comparisons, and remember to dovetail outcomes.

Using metaphors is not always smooth sailing, however. Let me describe one time a metaphor almost sank a seminar. I and some colleagues had just begun a new company, and we were conducting our first seminar in Chicago. I found myself in a difficult situation, shown here under "present state." I knew what my "desired state" was, but I was not quite sure of the best approach to use to get it.

Present State	*Desired State*
• I had a new, young assistant.	• Get him to stop sabotaging my efforts.
• He was skilled in some ways, but unskilled in others.	• Get him to begin supporting my efforts.
• We were teaching together.	
• He was sabotaging my teaching without knowing it.	

During my seminar, while the participants were creating metaphors, I made up a metaphor about Christopher Columbus. I wanted to gain my new assistant's understanding and support, so I wrote a metaphor about Chris and his young mate, who was an experienced sailor but knew nothing about navigation. The mate thought they were going to fall off the earth and was inciting the other sailors to mutiny. How could Columbus get this young mate to cooperate?

I wrote all this down in what I thought was my own notebook. It was actually my assistant's notebook. (My unconscious must have been desperate for a change in his behavior.) This is what I wrote:

Columbus Metaphor

Me	Christopher Columbus
assistant	mate
new	new
young	young
sabotage	inciting rebellion
together in seminar	together in boat
outcome: stop the behavior for both our good	*outcome*: stop the behavior for both our good

During my seminar lecture on metaphor, my assistant read my metaphorical notes. He became angry, not at the metaphor, not at my expressed outcome, but at being called "young." In spite of his anger, however, he stopped his subversive behavior and began cooperating, even supporting, my teaching; and the seminar improved greatly.

That night he confronted me about the metaphor. What could I say? He agreed with my outcome. I agreed not to call him "young." Then we sailed around the globe together, both of us believing in the power of metaphors.

Selecting Parallel Key Components

When you construct a complex metaphor, focus on one, two, three, four, five, or six elements intrinsic to both your current situation—your present state—and the one you want to be in—your desired state. Make a list of these elements. Then match the key components of these elements with a real experience or a make-believe tale. You can heavily disguise the elements because the unconscious mind is clever enough to strip away disguises with ease. The last part of the metaphor is always your outcome, disguised. The other person may choose not to go along with your outcome after listening to the metaphor, but it will take an effort to resist, as long as you are dovetailing.

Metaphors have a strong pull. If your outcome is not in direct conflict with your listener's outcome, s/he will tend to unpeel the disguise and go along with your purpose, with pleasure. "With pleasure" is the unexpected dividend of the metaphor. Metaphors are joyous ways to influence.

Some time ago, I received a letter from a business manager of a large corporation who asked me to design a metaphor for him. He had tried and had not been able to come up with one he liked. This was his situation: Because of an old policy in his company, individuals who were not doing a particularly good job continued to receive salary increases routinely while others, who were making outstanding contributions, were not receiving awards commensurate with their efforts. He had access to the president and wanted a metaphor, not too disguised.

So I told him about a farmer who had a barn in which a dozen or so mice had made themselves at home. The mice were a nuisance and were eating the grain supply. The farmer had six cats that were supposed to be mousers, but the mice kept multiplying. The cats lay around in the sun all day and partied all night, and the mice prospered.

Finally, a grey tabby caught a mouse and brought it to the farmer. He immediately poured thick cream into a saucer for the cat. The other cats had scanty rations that night, but the grey cat dined well. The next day the grey tabby caught three mice, and she was again rewarded by the farmer. By the third day the barn was free of mice. The farmer then moved the tabby into the kitchen, where her saucer was kept brimming with cream.

Let's look at how the key components in this metaphor match the key components in the business situation.

Parallel Key Components

People	*Cats*
not getting job done but getting rewarded	not catching mice but getting fed and partying all night
outcome: reward those who deserve reward	*outcome*: tabby moves into house and gets cream

The businessman used this metaphor with the president. A month later he called to say that his company was working on a new set of policies to recognize and reward employee contributions.

To help you remember the steps in building a complex metaphor, you can use the word "metaphor" as a mnemonic.

M   Match
E   Elements
T   That
A   Apply to
P   Present state/desired state
H   Hide them in a story
O   Organized around outcomes for
R   Receptive response

In constructing a metaphor, you must think the key elements through so that you know where you are—present state—and where you want to go—desired state.

Begin your metaphor with the situation you want to change, and end with the desired situation. When you think through this change, you may realize that you have experienced similar changes or know of similar situations in literature, history, or myth. By using these similar elements, you can produce your own metaphor. Once you begin thinking in metaphorical terms, you will become better and better at finding tales to fit your outcomes.

When you have selected the important elements in your metaphor, then decide how to disguise the parallel elements. The story you design will have to be appropriate to the setting, of course. You would not ordinarily tell a fairy tale to a board of directors. Yet I heard about a conflict between two departments of an international conglomerate that was solved by a metaphor about brown rabbits.

One department had been handling a particular situation in a foreign country for some years, but because of a certain crisis, another department moved in to help. The first department felt that its jurisdiction and ability to handle the crisis were being questioned and began to criticize the newcomer's efforts. The newcomer criticized back, and the conflict escalated. Then a clever storyteller related this tale to the heads of both departments.

A brown rabbit learned how to shoot a gun, and he wanted to hunt. He looked at an elephant and decided elephants were too big. He looked at a jaguar and decided jaguars were too fast. He decided to try out his gun on brown rabbits. He killed quite a number of brown rabbits. Then hunting season officially opened. There weren't too many brown rabbits left, and one of the first brown rabbits captured by a human rabbit hunter was our gun-toting friend. As the hunter trussed him up and took him away to the cooking pot, the rabbit lamented, "It's not fair. Why does everything happen to me?"

After hearing this story, the two groups began to work together.

Ted Tries to Be Subtle

Ted was division manager in a large petroleum company. His division's sole purpose was to design incompany programs for mainframe computers. Ted came to one of my seminars and told me he wanted a metaphor to explain a $200,000 overrun on a design for another division. In one week Ted had to meet with the other division manager, Walt, who had authorized the project. Not only was Ted $200,000 over budget but the program was not working. He would have to start again from scratch, and he needed a new budget allocation.

Ted had already dismissed the employee who had been primarily at fault for the fiasco, but as manager, he was responsible.

We played with ideas all week. By Friday, we had a fairly good metaphor about creating an innovative type of glider (Walt was a glider enthusiast) based on new aerodynamic principles; we included in our story unexpected glitches that had cost additional time and money. Ted would talk about how valuable the effort had been because of all the project staff had learned, even though the glider had to be redesigned.

Ted was a direct, straightforward person, but he had never had a work problem this serious before. And so, he thought a metaphor would be a better way to approach Walt than a more direct communication. (Remember, the power of a metaphor is that it speaks to the unconscious, and less directly, to the conscious mind.)

On Friday morning, we were to film Ted role-playing his meeting with Walt. As the camera began recording, Walt's surrogate looked up and greeted Ted, who had entered the pretend office. Ted was already nervous. He sat down in a chair, looked directly at "Walt," and announced, "I have a metaphor for you."

Your desired state. When you know the state you want to attain, you can organize the ending of your tale to describe it. The purpose of the metaphor is to invite your communication partner to join you in your desired state—a state you describe in such attractive terms that it becomes almost irresistible. But remember: A metaphor is an invitation, not a command. Whether your desired state will become a reality depends to a large degree on your skill in creating and telling your tale, which brings us to the last step in communicating with metaphors.

Response. The response you get will tell you whether or not your metaphor was successful. Sometimes the response will be slight, perhaps an almost imperceptible nod or a finger twitch, especially if it is coming from the unconscious. However, be assured that there will be a response.

If the response to your invitation is "no," reexamine your partner's outcome. Then go off and design another metaphor. People love stories. If the response is "yes," congratulate yourself on creating a complex metaphor that worked.

Remember, there is nothing new in the technique of metaphor. It has been used as a teaching and influencing tool since human beings began to use language to communicate.

Now that you understand how to design a metaphor, we are going to move on to look at the concept of congruence in depth. The first steps toward congruence were introduced in *Influencing with Integrity* and elicited many questions from readers who wanted to know how they could increase their congruence in business settings. Chapter 6 presents the next steps in the journey toward congruence and toward understanding the many facets of your essence.

Essence—our original face before we were born

POLARITIES

POLARITIES

This chapter is dedicated to Ms. Beulah Edinburg, who modeled the power of congruence in an adverse situation.

6 Communicating Congruently

What happens when you send double messages—when your words say one thing and your voice tone, facial expression, or body posture says the opposite? People do not believe you. Consciously or unconsciously (intuitively), they are picking up conflicting internal states, and they do not trust what you are saying. If you think you could have more impact, if you think you are not getting enough respect, if you find it difficult to convince people of the truth of your position, then you may be sending double messages— you may be incongruent.

Congruence, on the other hand, is a state of agreement and harmony. Congruence means that all your parts, your subpersonalities, are working in a unified way to achieve your objective. When you are congruent in your communication, all your subpersonalities are aligned with your outcome.

95

Actually, it is far easier to talk about the lack of congruence than about its presence. We have all come into contact with incongruent individuals, and sometimes we ourselves are incongruent. The stereotype of the used-car salesman is characterized by lack of congruence. The same goes for many other salespeople when they do not believe in their product or do not care about your outcome. Although you may not know exactly why, you simply do not trust certain people. Can you think of some incongruent people you have met?

Not all used-car salesmen are incongruent.

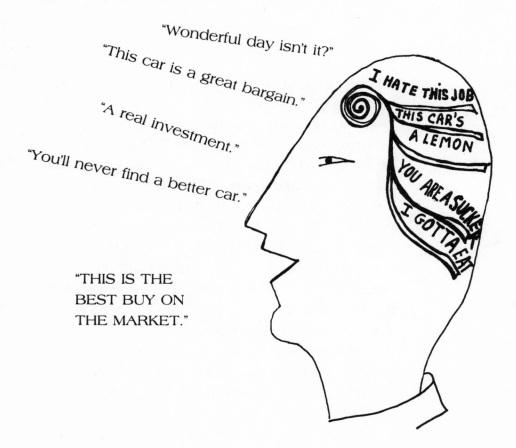

"Wonderful day isn't it?"

"This car is a great bargain."

"A real investment."

"You'll never find a better car."

"THIS IS THE BEST BUY ON THE MARKET."

I HATE THIS JOB
THIS CAR'S A LEMON
YOU ARE A SUCKER
I GOTTA EAT

Congruent salespeople speak and grow rich.

Politicians are often incongruent, and the ones who do not get elected are almost always so. Religious leaders sometimes lack congruence, especially if they are going through their own "dark night of the soul." People you instinctively do not believe, even though they are considered experts in their fields, are almost certainly incongruent within themselves. Can you think of times when you were incongruent and realized it, or someone pointed it out to you? Parents are often incongruent when they direct their children to do something they do not do themselves. Then the children get a mixed message about the worth of the activity. Remember the adage "Don't do as I do, do as I say"? It is no surprise that children often ignore this incongruent message.

Some incongruence is a normal part of human behavior. We all have dilemmas now and then.

Babies are congruent. Children are usually congruent until age five or so.

Here is a way for you to see yourself being blatantly incongruent. Once you are consciously aware of your incongruent mannerisms, it is easier to catch yourself and stop the behavior. Look in a mirror, try to speak convincingly to a pretend audience on the other side of the mirror about how delicious chocolate ice cream is when mixed with ketchup. Then tell your audience about your favorite dessert. Can you hear the difference in your voice? Can you see the difference in your mouth? Can you notice the difference in your gestures? Run through this a couple of times, and write down the differences.

Congruence is not a goal to reach, but a star to move toward.

Three Steps to Basic Congruence

1. Become familiar with the concept of congruence. Define the term for yourself in view of your own experiences.
2. Notice when you are congruent. "Te" will be apparent; events will be flowing with you, effortlessly.
3. Learn to recognize incongruent behaviors and the situations in which they occur.
   a. Spend time alone sorting out your priorities.
   b. Perhaps you need a Parts Party (see Appendix).

One Step to Advanced Congruence

1. Gradually extend the times of congruence in your life. In Zen this is called the path which is not a path.

Many different techniques can be used to attain a greater level of congruence. Here are a few:

- Ask one subpersonality to be in charge of congruence and to notify you when you are congruent and when you are not. Gain the part's acceptance of this task; a "yes" here is very important.
- Ask a close friend to tell you when you are congruent and when you are not.
- Spend 10 minutes each weekend playing back your week's movies, emphasizing the times you were congruent.
- If you recognize incongruence in your movies, change the scenes until you are congruent.
- Each time you look at your watch in the course of the day, ask yourself, "On a scale of 1 to 10, how do I rate on congruence?" Be easy on yourself. It takes time to get to 10.
- Design a personalized way to improve your congruence. When you have reached a plateau, come up with a new design to take you further.

OUR TWO BRAINS

Incongruence usually results from internal conflicts: One part of you wants one thing, and another part wants the opposite. Unless these "two minds" are reconciled, your words may be saying one thing and your voice tone and tempo the opposite. This leaves your audience confused as to your "real" message.

Some experts believe that these internal conflicts (both major and minor) result from our brain having two hemispheres, or sides—a left brain and a right brain—that process information in different ways. Other experts believe the learning processes of identification and introjection are the primary reasons we have internal conflicts. We will explore these two processes later in this chapter.

The experts seem to be having trouble deciding which side of the brain does what, but the latest conclusions are that the left side is verbal, linear, and sequential, and the right side is spatially oriented, holistic, and all-at-once. Because the two sides of the brain communicate with each other through the corpus callosum, and because many thinking activities use both sides of the brain, specialization is difficult to track. In this book we are less interested in what each side of the brain does than in the fact that we have two "computers." Our two brains process perceptions in two different ways, and they may come up with different conclusions, producing internal conflicts. Disagreement among these parts of our personality—our subpersonalities—is a major problem that causes incongruity, which, in turn, sabotages communication.

"There is a recent and very popular myth that has it that everything good must involve the right hemisphere. In fact, it is the *left* hemisphere that seems to be involved in happy and pleasant emotional experiences, and the right that is involved in negative feelings such as anger."
—*The Amazing Brain*

"We may then conclude that the individual with two intact hemispheres has the capacity for two distinct minds. This conclusion finds its experimental proof in the split-brain animal whose two hemispheres can be trained to perceive, consider, and act independently."
—*The Nature of Human Consciousness*

How can incongruity sabotage communication? Remember that communication is not limited to the words you use. It includes body posture, hand gestures, facial expressions, breathing rate, facial color, muscle tension, pulse rate, and more. Voice tone, volume, tempo, and timbre are vital parts of your communication. Any of these could reflect a subpersonality in conflict with your outcome and thus could contradict your verbal message by some observable behavior.

How can we reduce this incongruity and increase our personal power? Theories from gestalt psychology suggest that resolving conflicts between our conflicting parts and reaching at least temporary agreements as to outcomes will increase our effectiveness. For example, what if one part of you wants to go skiing, and another part wants to complete a report? A simple way to resolve this conflict is to assign a time schedule for each: Finish the report on Saturday, and ski on Sunday.

Intuition may be information stored in the unconscious.

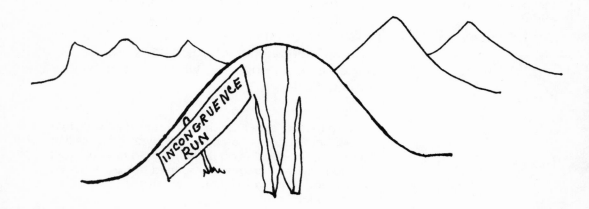

UNCONSCIOUS

CONSCIOUS

Because so many of our perceptions are unconscious, if a conflict exists, your communication partner will probably read the incongruence in one of your other body channels. That person may not know why s/he does not believe what you are saying, but will act on unconsciously perceived information. Because your whole message will be received intact, you would do well to have all your subpersonalities in agreement before you start to speak. Conflicting subpersonalities will sabotage each other verbally and nonverbally; Freudian slips are subpersonalities speaking up.

SUBPERSONALITIES AFFECT BEHAVIOR

Our behaviors are what make us interesting and effective participants in our world, and many of our behaviors reflect subpersonality conflicts. These conflicts are not necessarily all negative. They make us unique and many-faceted. They may also cause problems.

Personality	Subpersonality
The dynamic psyche that constitutes and animates the individual and makes his experience of life unique; the pattern of collective character, behavioral, temperamental, emotional, and mental traits of an individual.	One part of a total pattern of personality; often modeled on a parent or mentor. A subpersonality may be formed by identification or by introjection.

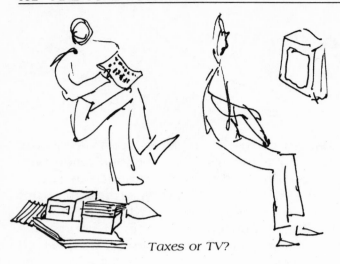

Taxes or TV?

Have you ever thought, "I need to work on my taxes," but were unable to concentrate? Or have you ever felt restless and unable to focus on the task at hand? You knew you must finish and yet—not today? Or have you ever said, "I'd like to take that transfer to Philadelphia, but on the other hand, I'd like to stay here in New York"? Perhaps this sounds familiar: "I'd really like to lose 10 pounds, but on the other hand, that cream pie looks too good to pass up"? The skinny you and the fat you are both inside struggling for control. One part of you wants to do one thing, and another part wants to do something else. Sometimes these opposing parts are called *polarities*.

Chances are that you have subpersonalities, whether you know it or not. Even if you are not accustomed to thinking in terms of subpersonalities, you have probably felt internal conflicts. Do you recognize these internal conflict dialogues: "Should I hire that person or not?" "Should I try for that promotion or not?" "Should I go to that party or not?"

You could think of each of these positions as being put forth by one part of your personality and being opposed by another part. Literally, of course, there is no real division; we are all of a piece. Even our two brains are connected and shuttle information back and forth.

New York or Philly?

Polarities are two subpersonalities that have opposite behaviors.

Fritz Perls's work in the sixties was based on the theory of conflicting subpersonalities, and he was able to assist people with dramatic personality changes, leading to more positive behaviors.

Some subpersonalities seem to be unacquainted with others and apparently unaware that they are in conflict. This conflict can result in an ongoing energy drain in a person who may not even realize that such a phenomenon is taking place.

Sometimes subpersonality conflicts can result in inexplicable behavior. Here are two examples, bizarre but true, that will give you a sense of how severe such conflicts and the resulting lack of communication can be.

A man in Baton Rouge, Louisiana, rang the doorbell of a certain house and politely requested his hat, which he had left the day before when he had raped the lady of the house. He was arrested. It seems that the part of his personality that liked the hat forgot to check with another part regarding past behavior.

The philosophy of dovetailing can keep you out of jail.

The Congruent Con Artist
A con artist who is even moderately congruent can swindle millions. Surprised? If so, you were assuming that congruence is honesty. It is not. And congruence without honesty means real trouble because it implies personal power with no brakes. Con artists are good examples of what can happen when a good tool is put to destructive use. If you fail to consider the other person's outcome in an interaction, you eventually pay a heavy price.

In another city, a bank robber wrote a demand note on the back of his deposit slip. Not only did the deposit slip have his account number on it, but he had written his name and address as well. If these behaviors do not indicate a lack of communication between subpersonalities, I do not know how to explain them.

IDENTIFICATION AND INTROJECTION

Subpersonalities may be formed by the processes of identification and introjection. One way human beings learn is by identifying with others they consider powerful. Once you identify with a person, you learn to be like that person. Do you remember pretending you were your mother or your father, or a favorite teacher, or a popular sports figure, or an actress? You were learning how to behave the way those models behaved. When children and teenagers emulate grownups, they are said to be identifying with their models. In fact, this kind of learning is called *identification*.

You can be successful and incongruent, but you may not enjoy your success.

Identification is a normal, natural way to learn. Another natural way to learn is introjection, which is similar to identification, but here the learned behaviors are outside the learner's awareness. Fritz Perls defines "introjection" as the "mechanism whereby we incorporate into ourselves standards, attitudes, ways of acting and thinking which are not truly ours." By "not truly ours," Perls means that the introjects are unconscious. These standards, attitudes, and behaviors do not become conscious parts of our personalities; these "pieces" of personality become the subpersonalities that often operate outside our awareness.

One thing you should know about subpersonalities—those often conflicting internal drives: They are often introjected parts of your parents. Have you ever heard yourself speaking to your children and suddenly realized you sounded like one of your parents?

A professor at an art college gave a speech on the importance of spontaneity for creative thinking while standing in a military parade position the entire time he spoke.

A teacher, turned investment counselor, extolled the benefits of an investment as she nervously snapped and unsnapped the lock on her purse.

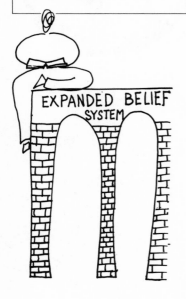

Most of us seem to have whole sets of behaviors that take over in response to certain situations. We wonder later, "Now why did I do that?"

One day my son reached for a piece of fried chicken, already placed on the table for dinner, as he walked though the dining room. I said, "No, you don't. You wait for dinner to eat that." Then I realized that was my mother speaking. I really did not care if he munched on fried chicken in the 10 minutes before dinner. I suddenly remembered how long 10 minutes seems to a child, and I called him back and give him the chicken leg.

Successful women in business sometimes use introjects from their fathers. I gave a presentation recently to a group of women who were fascinated by the material; yet two of the three remained distant, cold, formal, and almost negative. The third did not have this business-is-serious-business introject and she showed her interest. I warmed to her and gave a much better presentation than I would have if she had not been there. Communication is a feedback system; we affect one another. The distance the two "serious" businesswomen established deprived all of us of our best interaction. Thinking about the presentation later, I wondered if the two women were modeling "serious" businessmen—perhaps their fathers.

Introjects are actually learned automatic behaviors all bundled together and triggered by particular stimuli. When one pattern conflicts with another, the result is often incongruence.

EXPERIENCES + INTROJECTS = BELIEF SYSTEMS
(other's beliefs)

When we are sending double messages, one of them from our introjects, we do not know that we are caught up in the behaviors of the models we have identified with. Introjects are powerful and difficult to control, and they may conflict with our major outcomes. Becoming aware of our own introjects is an important step in achieving congruence. The reframing exercise in Chapter 7 will help you uncover your own introjects and the subpersonalities they spawn.

"Shoulds" and "should nots" are indicators of introjects.

Ed Discovers an Introject

Ed arrived at the first session of an introject awareness group wondering why he had come. He had had 23 years of psychoanalysis, was coleading an encounter group, and felt he knew all he needed to know about how his psyche worked. He had already spent a fortune finding himself. He said he was acutely aware that it was crazy to experiment with his own psyche after all the expensive training it had already undergone. He was here in a search for congruence.

Once the session began, Ed dived in with his usual enthusiasm and served as a potent stimulus for those with less experience in digging around in their unconscious. The introject that showed up again and again in Ed's workshop sessions was "keep 'em laughing." Ed found this introject surprising. He knew he could be funny; he had earned survival money for his family doing witty improvisations at parties. What he did not know was that he *had* to leave them laughing—every person, every time. He was constantly pushed by this internal, energy-draining rule.

It was especially difficult to "keep 'em laughing" when his chosen profession—acting—did not support him financially or emotionally. He was always scrounging for bit parts, begging money for amateur theater groups, and just generally never hitting the Broadway jackpot. No star billing for Ed—just small print on the back of programs, and having to make them laugh as well.

It was clear as the sessions unfolded that Ed's upbringing and the admonition to make them laugh were somehow connected. This interconnected web kept him tangled, captive—away from what he had wanted for years: to be a successful, rich, acclaimed actor.

A double bind = horns of a dilemma = polarities in conflict: damned if you do and damned if you don't.

The importance of this double bind—a fear of failure and a compulsion to make them laugh—seemed to have eluded 23 years of psychoanalysis. During the

workshop, Ed made a breakthrough in his own understanding of his conflicting subpersonalities. His fear
of failure had neatly sabotaged his desire for success.
His need to "keep 'em laughing," no matter how
depressed he felt over his career, kept him incongruent and less than believable when auditioning.

If Ed had told me at the start of the workshop session about his years of self-exploration with psychia-
trists, I would have advised him not to join the group;
we would probably have nothing new for him. To
this day, I underestimate the ability of introjects to
hide.

A week after the workshop ended, Ed auditioned
for a major role in a Broadway play and got it, and he
has been on Broadway ever since. Although your
introjects may not be keeping you from a starring role
on Broadway, they may be keeping you from gaining
all the success you deserve.

Introject

A standard, an attitude, or a behavior that has been
"borrowed" from someone else and is operating on
an unconscious level in opposition to our essence—
our real self

Remember that subpersonalities are formed primarily through the process of introjection, and introjects
are unconscious. This means that, like Ed, you may
not know about some of your subpersonalities. Once
you become aware that you have subpersonalities,
begin to notice any surprising reactions. These may
signal subpersonality conflicts. You can then decide
whether your subpersonalities and their behaviors
are useful. If they are useful, do not disturb. But if
the behavior of a subpersonality is a problem for you,
you need to learn to manage it in a useful way. Once
you are aware of your subpersonalities, you can find
creative ways to harness their energy for your outcomes. The Parts Party in the Appendix is an exam-

ple of how to explore your subpersonalities and how to resolve their conflicts so you will be congruent in your behavior.

CONGRUENCE:
THE INTEGRATION OF PARTS

When individuals are congruent—when other people believe them, trust them, recognize their authenticity— they are powerful people, whatever their role in life. Congruence offers many advantages, for you and for those who interact with you.

Congruence fine-tunes your outcomes. The search for congruence forces you to become aware of both your conscious and your unconscious outcomes. When we are not consciously aware of our out- comes, our unconscious often dictates, and its instinctual needs will push for satisfaction. If we do not know consciously what we want, our uncon- scious will guide our selection of perceptions. Then, through our thinking processes, we organize those perceptions in order to satisfy our unconscious drive.

When unconscious and conscious outcomes are in opposition, the unconscious usually wins. However, when the two work together, your unconscious assets are at the disposal of your conscious out- comes. These two make a powerful pair.

UNCONSCIOUS

CONSCIOUS

7 ± 2 bits of infor- mation—current theory of how much the conscious mind can handle at one moment

Congruence gives your words impact. The end result of congruence is that when you have something important or interesting to say, all your subpersonalities will know it and will support your words. You will send a single message, and this focus is forceful. Having congruence means you will not have to talk loudly to get the attention of your listeners.

Congruence and integrity are natural partners. A synonym for integrity is honesty. Remember that congruence means all your parts are working toward your outcome in a unified way. Unless we have been terribly stunted by our life experiences, we have an honest part and a fairness part. Incorporating attributes of honesty and fairness in our interactions increases our personal satisfaction as we continue to move toward congruence and integrity.

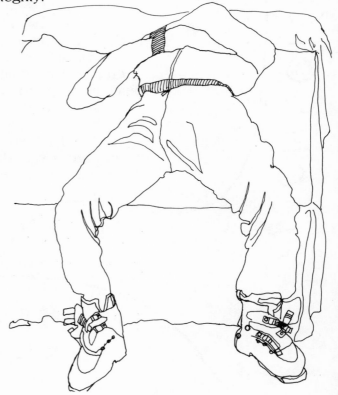

Congruence means peace of mind. When your subpersonalities agree about your outcomes, you feel a notable sense of purpose and contentment. Some people achieve a second-rate version of this feeling by giving over their lives to an institution or to a person who makes their decisions for them. This second-rate peace of mind is what creates cults. In my opinion this is a cop-out. Our brains are designed to make decisions. If you are congruent, honest with yourself, and use integrity in your decision making, you will be at peace with yourself.

COMMUNICATING CONGRUENTLY 111

Congruence turns errors into experiments. Congruence means you do not have to worry about your slip showing—Freudian or silk. Further, you do not have to be concerned about making a mistake. When you are congruent, a mistake is simply an attempt that is unsuccessful; it only points out the need to do something else, to try another approach. When you have done the best you can, you can stop labeling events "mistakes"; instead, label them "experiments." Some moves work; some do not. If you prefer to be engaged in experiments rather than mistakes, then congruence is the way.

Congruence means you do not have to worry about your slip showing—Freudian or silk.

Freudian Slips

This analysis suggests we leave a wide margin for terror (error).

I recommend that we enter into an argument (agreement) on these issues.

This is a cost-elective (-effective) solution.

Verbal Congruence

In many communication interactions, the tone of voice carries the real message. When your tone says, "This is not really important" even though your words say, "This is really important," your communication is incongruent. And your listener will hear "not important" just from the tone of your voice.

When you can use voice tone, tempo, and timbre in ways that support and reinforce the focus of your words, you will be congruent. When you are congruent, your voice will reflect the working together of all your parts, and you will be far more effective in your communication.

Congruence increases credibility. Being even moderately congruent increases your credibility with others. Early in my career I conducted a training for a competitor who said he was curious about our new skills. I think he was looking for congruence.

This competitor was an outstanding business consultant on the East Coast. He had attained a level of congruence that had given him credibility in 400 of the Fortune 500 companies. These firms paid him for his services, and well. Yet this man was riddled with internal conflicts, apparent to those with little training. He would shake his head from left to right as he stated a "clear" position. He would laugh at inappropriate moments. He talked of honesty and paid me less than agreed. I have to admit that I found it surprising that he was as successful as he was. Could it be that there is so little congruence in the business world that even the modest amount he had attained went a long way?

Shortly after the seminar, he changed professions. I have often wondered if this switch was the result of insights into his own double messages. He made some progress in the course of the seminar, but he needed more than three days' work.

An investment broker once took me to lunch to convince me to sell my options on a stock I owned. All during lunch he watched everyone in the room except me and never heard my well-thought-through investment plans. As we said good-bye, he asked, looking over my shoulder, "So you'll call me about those options, right?" He never got a call.

Knowing yourself means knowing all your subpersonalities.

Congruence means you have learned to manage yourself. You set outcomes and get out of your own way. You no longer sabotage your best-laid plans. And when you can manage yourself, you are ready to manage others.

*Potential
energy*

*Baseline of feel-
ing normally
good*

*Where many
business peo-
ple spend their
workday*

Congruence results in energy and exhilaration. For most of us, conflicts among our subpersonalities are so painful and disturbing that we repress them—we keep them from our conscious awareness. This repression, as Sigmund Freud pointed out, requires a lot of energy. In spite of our intense desire for repression, certain facets of the conflicts continue to show up in our behaviors. For example, if we have a love/hate relationship with our job, we may work long hours, strive mightily, then "forget" an important meeting. By becoming aware of our internal conflicts, we can release the mental energy we have been using for repression, work out some internal negotiations, and use the released energy in our lives.

Once you have experienced the ease, energy, and excitement of being focused in one direction, you may become addicted to the feeling. You no longer have the energy drain that results from repressing conflicts. You no longer take six steps in one direction, then six steps backward. You have the wonderful feeling that comes from all your parts working together smoothly, giving you peak performance and exhilaration. Some people get this feeling from skiing, from throwing clay on a potter's wheel, from racing boats or cars. Quite simply, when body and mind are working together, when all your attention is focused—that is congruence.

Let's work together.

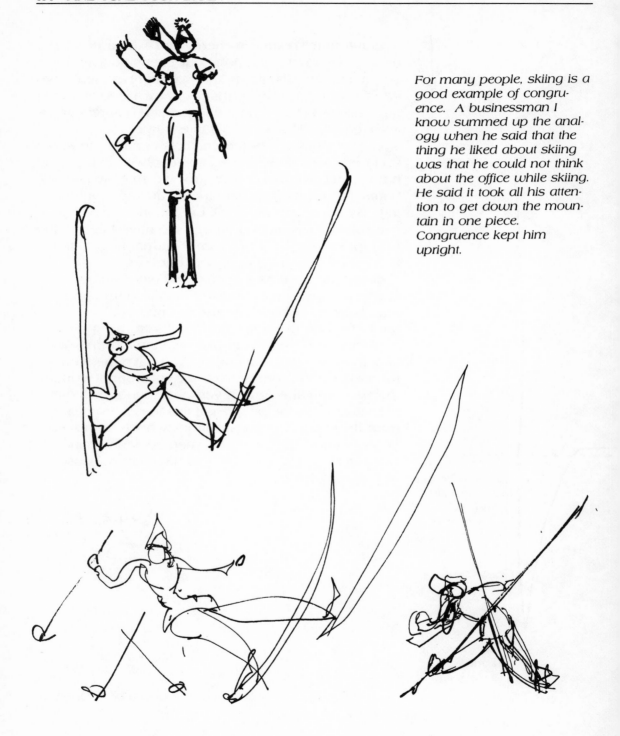

For many people, skiing is a good example of congruence. A businessman I know summed up the analogy when he said that the thing he liked about skiing was that he could not think about the office while skiing. He said it took all his attention to get down the mountain in one piece. Congruence kept him upright.

Congruence is so powerful that the proper use of it is as important as possessing it.

Congruence is so rare that its presence alone ensures personal power. I am referring not only to the power attached to a prominent position, such as president of the United States, but to quiet, composed, even understated personal power.

I have been fascinated by personal power for many years. Who has it? Who does not? Is it based on money, on job position in a hierarchy? Is there a personal power that has nothing to do with these outside trappings?

As I have implied throughout this chapter, a certain kind of personal power cannot be bought or based on a title. I have known a few people who have it. From studying them, I now believe congruence is the foundation of personal power.

Suppose you agree that congruence sounds like a fine thing to have. How do you get it? The next chapter will give you additional skills and teach you some things about yourself. You may even coax some of your introjects out of hiding.

Once you have experienced the ease, energy, and excitement of being focused in one direction, you may become addicted to the feeling.

Well......at least we got to name the animals.

7
A New Frame

Sometimes you know what you want, but your actions keep you from getting it. In other words, you have a behavior that blocks you from obtaining your outcomes. For example, let's say you want a promotion, and one of the prerequisites for promotion is that all your projects have to be in on time. You know that, but you continually finish your work a day late, a week late, a month late. You may not be consciously aware of the conflict, but your behavior indicates that a conflict is indeed present. Part of you wants to complete projects on schedule, and part of you does not.

The key to changing this behavior is finding out the intent of the part that is sabotaging you—in this case, the part that always finishes late. Subpersonalities try to protect you in some way. The part that is turning in the projects late is protecting you, but from what? You need to know more about this protection. If you can find out the intent of the behavior, you can start functioning in a way that will gain you the promotion. You will begin to communicate the message, congruently, that you do deserve a promotion. Or once you know the intent of your "Late" part, you may decide you do not want the promotion. Then you will be congruent about that.

Procrastination is worth a reframe.

It is difficult for your conscious mind to know the intent of a behavior. Your Late part's intent may be to protect you from working too closely with an irascible supervisor or to make you so miserable that you will look for a more promising position outside the company. Whatever the part's specific intent, you can be sure it has one. Once your apparently contradictory part has new behaviors that will satisfy its protective intent, that part will allow you to function in a manner congruent with your most important outcomes.

You can find out the intent of a contradicting part, an unruly subpersonality, and through a process called *reframing*, you can learn to satisfy the intent in another way—a way that is not destructive to your outcomes.

Reframes

Two distinctly different mental processes have both come to be known as reframes. This is somewhat understandable because, in both mental processes, the "intention" behind a certain behavior is the key to a change.

Simple reframes are used in handling objections in a meeting or during a sales call. In a simple reframe, the person doing the reframe has to guess at the intention behind the other person's objection. In a complex reframe, used mainly to change unwanted behaviors, such as procrastination and overspending, the subpersonality involved supplies the intention. The person wishing to make a change provides all the information and basically does the work.

Quick Reframes

It's a hot day.
Reframe: Yes! Let's go swimming. The water will be perfect.

My boss quit.
Reframe: Wonder if the new one will be easier to work with.

I have a run in my stocking.
Reframe: Good excuse to take them off and go bare-legged—so comfortable.

My plane will be 3 hours late.
Reframe: What a good time to catch up on paperwork. Do you have enough in your briefcase to keep you busy? Or would you like to hear the details of my solution to that Detroit snafu?

Reframes in Sales

This car costs almost twice as much as the one I'm driving now.
Reframe: Yes, it does; and it will still be running in five years, which means cost per year will be way down, and maintenance will be less. And wait till your friends see you in a Porsche.

This watch looks fragile.
Reframe: It is delicate-looking on your wrist, and the craftsmanship is superb.

That's an expensive copier.
Reframe: The initial cost may seem higher. Let me show you our excellent maintenance schedule, and you will see how infrequently service is required.

Reframing is a useful way to introduce your subpersonalities to one another.

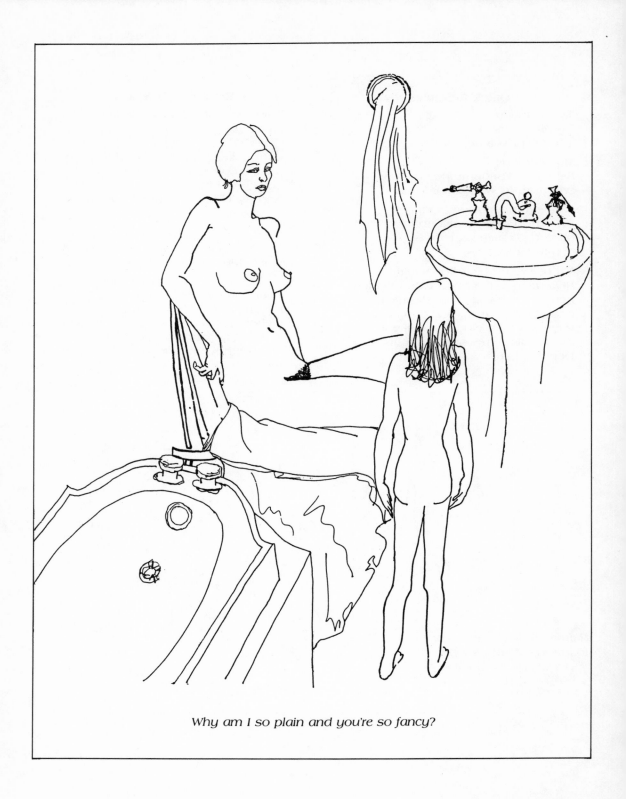

Why am I so plain and you're so fancy?

REFRAMING

This powerful technique developed, as far as I can tell, from "hot seat" gestalt. Fritz Perls's videotapes show him eliciting his clients' intentions, although his approach was less focused than the reframing technique.

The first published version of reframing that I know of was in Leslie Cameron-Bandler's book *They Lived Happily Ever After*. Since then, John Grinder and Richard Bandler published a book called *Reframing* with many variations of the basic steps.

Reframing can be done with a friend. Find someone you trust, and have him/her read the following directions to you. If you do not wish to talk during this process, your friend should be observant enough to know when you have completed each step. Or you may prefer to signal when you are ready for the next step. Choose a quiet place to go through these steps so you will not be interrupted.

Here is a mnemonic to help you through the sequence of steps.

R Recognize the part causing the unwanted behavior.

E Express appreciation to the part for past service. (This may be difficult.)

F Find out the intent of the behavior.

R Request your Creative part to find three new ways to satisfy the intent.

A Ask the part causing the unwanted behavior to agree to try the three new ways before using the old unwanted behavior.

M Make sure all parts agree on the new learning, the new behaviors.

E Ecology check. Will the new ways fit in with your life?

Now select a behavior that you would like to change, and let's begin fine-tuning this process.

122 FINE TUNE YOUR BRAIN

Recognize the part causing the unwanted behavior.
Even if you are not sure you have subpersonalities,
for the sake of achieving congruence *pretend* the
unwanted behavior is being caused by a subpersonality of yours. Identify the part causing the behavior
by focusing your attention on the behavior until you
get a mental image, a distinct feeling, or words. Give
that part a name. Close your eyes and begin an internal dialogue with that part of your personality.

First, ask the part if it would be willing to communicate with you. In response, you may get a body
sensation, such as a relaxed chest, or some other
indication of agreement. You may even hear a "yes"
from the internal tapes most of us carry around.
There will almost always be some kind of response.
If not, assume that silence means "yes."

Express appreciation to the part for past service.
In respectful tones, still in internal dialogue, tell the
part that you appreciate all the ways it has tried to
protect you. Take a moment to feel this appreciation.
If the part has made you gain 200 pounds, this may
take some effort. Remember that the part cares nothing about your weight; it cares only about protecting
you. You can appreciate what a good job the part
has done without being grateful for the form it took.
Very definitely, 200 pounds represents a lot of
protection.

Find out the intent of the behavior. Ask the part very gently and courteously to tell you the intent behind the behavior. The intent is the objective, the purpose of the offensive behavior, as viewed by the part itself. You will probably get an answer in feelings, pictures, or sounds. If, for some reason, you do not get an answer, then you can make some guesses and ask for a "yes" or "no" response from the part.

It is more effective if the part comes up with its intent because the intent is usually a total surprise to your conscious mind. If you receive a "no" to all guesses and the intent is very important to you, you might wish to get some professional help with reframing. However, in my experience, 90 percent of those who try can determine the intent without additional help. Be careful about learning the intent and dismissing it as "absurd." The intent does *not* seem absurd to the part protecting you. Once you know the intent, thank the part, and ask it to wait around while you get in touch with your Creative part.

Request your Creative part to find three new ways to satisfy the intent. If you do not have a Creative part, how about a Problem-Solving part, or a higher self, or some other part that you go to when you really need help? If you do not have such a part, pretend. Going through the motions works fine.

Ask your Creative part to come up with three new behaviors that will satisfy the intent and not include the unwanted behavior. In seven years of working with this step, I have never found anyone who could not find at least two behaviors. If only two behaviors come to mind, then you can ask your Creative part to continue working on new behaviors and let you know when it has them. Once you have the three new behaviors, thank your Creative part.

Ask the part causing the unwanted behavior to agree to try new ways before the old way. Now ask your sabotaging part, which has been waiting, if it is willing to try out the new behaviors before it resorts to the unwanted behavior. If it signals "yes," you are almost finished. If it responds "no," reassure the part that you are not taking away the possibility of using the unwanted behavior. You simply want the part to try out the new behaviors *before* the unwanted behavior. This will usually do the trick. You must get a positive "yes." If for some reason you do not, ask the Creative part to work with the stuck part to come up with alternative behaviors.

Make sure all parts agree on the new learning, the new behaviors. Check internally to make sure all your subpersonalities will go along with the new behaviors. If any part objects, use REFRAME again for this new part. Start this time with finding the intent of the objection (the F in REFRAME) expressed by the new part that has just spoken up.

When all parts agree, thank the part responsible for the past unwanted behavior for being cooperative. Then ask that part to get together with the Creative part so they are touching each other—perhaps a hand-shake or a hug. Sometimes, parts dance a jig together. Have fun noticing what happens when you release the energy of these parts who have been defending their positions. Then, ask them to help each other satisfy the intent in the future.

Ecology check. Finally, mentally check the important people and activities in your life to be sure that the changes that stem from your use of the new behaviors will be completely positive. If you gain confidence and, as a result, tell off your boss and lose your job, you may want to reconsider how you are planning to use this new confidence. In short, be sure the new learnings are ecologically balanced.

As a final step, bring all your parts back inside, and return to the here and now. You have been on a journey deep inside your own psyche. Give yourself time to return to your daily activities. Some quiet time would be useful and productive now.

Roger's Reframe

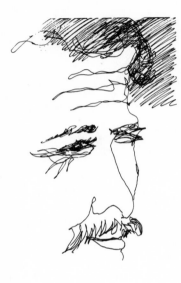

Here is an example of how a reframe helped Roger, a very successful sales representative, to sell himself. For seven years Roger had been a top sales-person for his company. Now he wanted to start his own business, leading sales seminars. He had been great at selling his company's products; but he discovered he was terrible at selling himself.

I asked Roger to get in touch with his Failure-in-Sales part. Failure responded immediately with an internal voice. "Yes, I'm here. What do you want?"

I instructed Roger to tell Failure that he appreciated how hard Failure had been working to keep him from selling. Roger choked and said, "I can't say that. I hate it."

"Take a deep breath. The part is trying to protect you in some way. You can appreciate that he is trying to do this."

"OK, Failure, thanks for trying to protect me. Let's work out a new behavior."

Roger, listening to his internal voice, looked shocked. "He's scared. He doesn't want a new behavior. He says he's doing fine, and he doesn't need any help."

"Good. Reassure him that you are going to help him do an even better job at protecting you."

"His voice has stopped quivering. He'll listen, but he's not sure he'll agree."

"Great. Now ask Failure what he's protecting you from."

Short pause. "He doesn't want me hurt. If I sell my

sales seminar and it fails, I would be very hurt and disappointed." Roger's voice was shaky and incredulous.

"Thank Failure for communicating with you, and reassure him once more."

Roger did this and then waited. We were working in front of a group, and the entire group seemed to be holding their breath. "Roger," I said, "take a deep breath." Everyone took a deep breath.

"Now, would you ask your Creative self to join us?"

"I don't think I have a Creative self."

"How about a Problem-Solving self?"

"Oh, yes, I do have one of those."

"Is he here?"

"Yes."

"Ask your Problem-Solving self to find a few ways to protect you from failing if you sell a seminar."

Long pause, then, "OK, I have four ways."

"Do you mind telling us what they are?"

"Sure, I'll tell you. If the first run is not great, I'll get feedback and change the seminar so it is great. That's one. I've been successful in the past at whatever I did; I will remember this every day. That's two. I will attend five sales seminars given by competitors to be sure mine are better. That's three. And I'll do a freebee for friends to get additional feedback about any changes I make. That's four."

"Good. Now ask Failure if he is willing to try out these new behaviors."

"Yes, he says, but he's not sure they'll work."

"Right. But he is willing to try them?"

"Yes."

"Now see if any other part objects to the new learning."

There was a long pause. Then Roger looked embarrassed. "Well, yes, there is another part that will not agree."

"What is that part's name?"

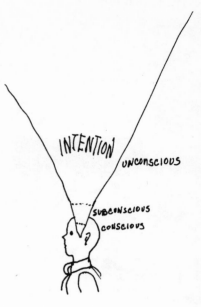

BLOCKING PARTS

Roger's
archetypal
subpersonalities:
Failure
Problem-Solving
Chance

Pause. "Chance. He's my Risk-Taking part. He joined the Army at 15. He doesn't want to go through all four steps. He wants to go ahead now."

"Thank Chance for speaking up."

"OK. He's dumbfounded. He's never been appreciated before. He likes it."

"Now ask him his intent in rushing you into the seminar business."

"He knows I can do it well, even without all that practice. He's impatient to get going. He's wearing running shoes."

"Ask him to wait while we talk to your Problem-Solving part."

"He says, 'OK, but hurry up.' He's impatient."

"I know. Is your Problem-Solving part ready with three behaviors for Chance?"

Short pause. "Yes"

"What are they?"

"First, Chance can be in charge of speed, so I'll move right along in finishing all four steps. He can also be in charge of taking risks while I'm doing those four steps. Chance can also be in charge of new learning while I'm getting ready to go."

"Has Chance heard these?"

"Yes."

"Will he agree?"

"He doesn't understand what new learning has to do with risk."

"Can you make the connection for him?"

"Yes."

"What does he say?"

"He's not very enthusiastic about the new learning."

"Will he agree?"

"He'll try it."

"Good. Now is there any other part that objects?"

"No objections."

"Good. Have all your parts—Chance included—shake hands, and bring them back inside you. We're finished."

Roger's fear of failure was the most important stumbling block to his success. By bringing this fear to his conscious awareness, he was able to reconcile the subpersonalities involved so they were willing to support one another.

The good intent of a subpersonality may cause behavior you do not want—behavior that may be blocking your career, affecting your relationships, even damaging your health. By reframing, you can get your parts to negotiate with one another and come up with creative alternatives to the unwanted behavior. This technique offers exciting insights into the causes of our conflicts, so be ready for some surprises.

INTENT IN ILLNESS

A physician named Georg Groddeck, a contemporary of Freud, first gave me the idea of looking for "intent" in illness. I read *The Book of the It* years ago and never forgot his theory that illness is a creative way for the personality to express itself.

Groddeck called the life force the *It*. He wrote: "The *It* is ambivalent, making mysterious, but deep-meaning, play with will and counter-will, with wish and counter-wish, driving the sick man into a dual relationship with his doctor so that he loves him as his best friend and helper, yet sees in him a menace to that artistic effort, his illness."

Let me give you a personal example of an interesting "intent" I turned up in one of my own malaises. This story may be difficult to believe, but Clarke's third law states, "Any sufficiently advanced technology is indistinguishable from magic." Reframing seems to produce magic tricks, as my own experience demonstrated.

Magic in Hong Kong

I went to Hong Kong to adopt a baby girl. In order for the transaction to be legal, the child's grandfather, who was her legal guardian, had to give her to me personally. The baby was ten days old and had been in the hospital nursery since birth. I was visiting her in the hospital twice a day, but she needed a lot more holding and cuddling. Cuddling was distinctly absent from the hospital routine.

On Thursday night the grandfather agreed that I could take the baby from the nursery on Saturday. I spent all day Friday buying baby things. I was in a hotel, so I needed lots of stuff—bottles, diapers, clothes, and so forth. When I came home from shopping, I had a terrible sore throat and was sure it was a strep infection. I know that newborns cannot tolerate strep germs; in fact, strep infections are sometimes fatal to them. For the baby's sake I simply could not take her from her grandfather's arms if I had strep throat.

When I returned to the hotel, I put down my shopping bags, sat down on the sofa, and asked, "Unwanted Behavior, why the strep? What is the intent?"

I got no response, so I went to a tried-and-true formula. I focused on my sore throat and said, "OK, Throat, I know you are trying to protect me, and I do appreciate it. But what is the intent?"

The answer was not sharp and clear, but I finally got it. Fuzzy, half-formed thoughts swarmed around. The message was that a part of me did not want to take charge of a baby at my age. Another part was concerned about my freedom; and another, about my new business, which was just beginning to succeed.

I thought I had worked these feelings through months ago, but I had not. I thanked the Strep part, which was difficult to do. I got out my Creative self, and we worked out three ways I could keep my freedom, continue to work, and have time for a child. None of this information was new to my conscious mind, but the Strep part had either not known about it or had been unconvinced that the planned behaviors would keep the Working part protected. The key to changing Strep was to hire a weekend nurse when I needed one. This entire process took about 40 minutes. At the end my throat still hurt, but less.

By morning I had no soreness at all. I met the grandfather, and he handed Kathryn over to me at the hospital at 10 a.m. I cuddled her all the way back to the hotel, and she loved it.

Opposite:

A visual metaphor for reframing. First picture has only an eye. Each additional frame includes new components—more options.

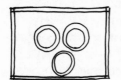

Reframing and similar powerful techniques raise provocative questions. After years of using such techniques successfully, I still do not know why they work. I have read much about the new discoveries regarding brain function, and I still have many unanswered questions. The following chapters deal with some of these issues—new and old discoveries about the brain, new skills for using resource states, and ways to replace an unwanted learned response with an acceptable new response. We'll start with questions to which we do not have answers.

Reframing has some interesting uses. How many do you suppose you can find?

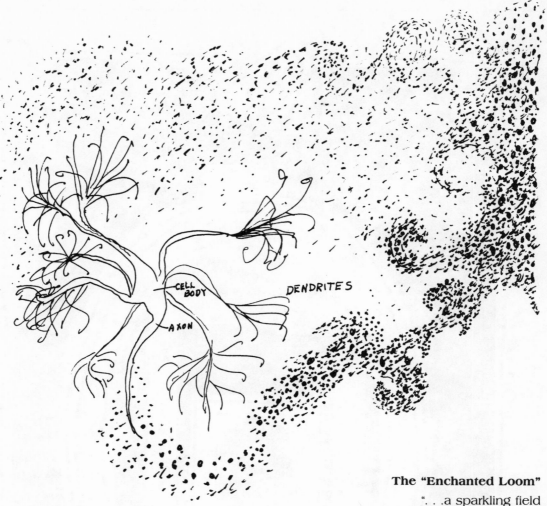

CELL BODY

AXON

DENDRITES

The "Enchanted Loom"

". . .a sparkling field
of rhythmic flashing points
with trains of traveling
sparks hurrying hither and thither.
The brain is waking and with it the mind is returning.
It is as if the Milky Way entered upon some cosmic dance.
Swiftly
the (cortex) becomes an enchanted loom where millions of flashing shuttles
weave a dissolving pattern, always a meaningful pattern though never an abiding one;
a shifting harmony of sub-patterns.
Now as the waking body arouses,
sub-patterns of this great harmony of activity
stretch down into the unlit tracks (of the lower brain).
Strings of flashing and traveling sparks engage the links of it."
—Charles Sherrington, *Man on His Nature*

8
Learning About Learning: A Brain Celebration

Why are some of us more intelligent than others? Why does a certain response become habitual for a certain stimulus? Why do we learn a phobic response in a few seconds and never forget it? Why do some people learn faster than others? Why do some people have learning disabilities, even though all parts of their brain appear to be intact? These are just some of the questions about the brain and its functions for which we do not have answers.

Karl Spenser Lashley spent 30 years studying the brain and then wrote:

> This series of experiments has yielded a good bit of information about what and where the memory trace is not. It has discovered nothing directly of the real nature of the engram. I sometimes feel, in reviewing the evidence of the localization of the memory trace, that the necessary conclusion is that learning just is not possible.

Lashley wrote this in 1950, and since then, brain scientists have learned a lot about learning—more than we can cover here. However, some of their findings will be useful for you to know about as we look at the advanced change techniques in later chapters. The unknowns and the knowns weave a tapestry almost as fascinating as the "enchanted loom" itself.

Provocative information arises from new research in psychology, biology, and new interrelated disciplines. A headless locust can still learn to position its leg in a certain way to avoid electric shock. A frog with an eye implanted upside down can learn to see right side up; yet another frog that received the implant just a few hours later can never make the change and lives in an upside-down world. The more research science undertakes, the more mysteries are revealed about our learning processes.

Engram—a stabilized pattern of response in the brain

A Note from the Author

In learning, in remembering, we are often dealing with mysteries. The processes of the brain, the patterning of an engram and what stabilizes it for short- and long-term recall, the ways we learn, are largely unknown.

In this chapter I have carefully separated knowns and unknowns, and labeled theories as such. Some of the ideas presented here may be outside the current mainstream of neurophysiological theory. I am including them as I search for a way to explain the magical effects of change techniques like reframing—techniques that appear to use the natural processes of the brain to bring about positive behavioral change. If you would like to study standard theories of brain neurology, here are three recommended texts:

Human Neuropsychology by Henry Hecaen and Martin L. Albert.

Clinical Neuropsychology, edited by Kenneth M. Heilman and Edward Valenstein

Principles of Behavioral Neurology, edited by M. M. Mesulam.

Parts of this chapter are quite technical. You will not need this information to understand and use the techniques in the chapters that follow.

LEARNING: SIMPLE AND COMPLEX

Simple learning is called stimulus-response, or habit learning. Responding to your given name is an example of stimulus-response. Certain aspects of complex learning are known as cognitive memory learning. The memory of your wedding day, with all its emotional overtones, is an example of cognitive memory. Each of these types of learning may be stored as either short-term or long-term memory.

Neurons in the brain

Short-Term Memory

Short-term memory is the mechanism we use when we look up an unknown telephone number in the phone book, walk over to the phone, and dial the number. J. C. Eccles, a neurophysiologist who won the Nobel Prize in medicine and physiology in 1963, has this to say about short-term memory:

> It is generally supposed that the recall of a memory involves the replay in an approximate manner of the neuronal events that were originally responsible for the experience being recalled. There is no specially difficult problem with short-term memories (for a few seconds). It can be conjectured that this is effected by the neural events continuing during the verbal or pictorial rehearsal. The distinctive patterns of modular activity . . . thus continue to recirculate for the whole duration of these brief memories and are available for read-out.

Short-term memory holds only 5 to 10 bits of information at a time, and usually for no more than 20 seconds. Consolidation of short-term memory into long-term memory requires time without interference, calcium, and a new protein, but what else it requires is not known. Although fascinating pieces of the puzzle are materializing, we do not know how we learn or how or what we remember, and sometimes it seems we do not know *what* we need to learn.

Short-term memory keeps neurons activated for the duration of the memory.

"Like understanding the origins of the universe and the physical principles of energy and matter, understanding the brain is one of the great challenges of mankind. It is, so far as we know, the most highly organized three-pound bundle of matter in the universe."

—Inside the Brain

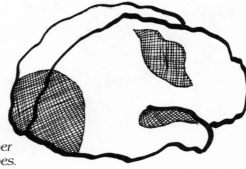

Short-term memory seems to involve the parietal, upper temporal, and occipital lobes.

Long-Term Memory

The brain seems to have a limitless and enduring capacity for storing our life experiences. Long-term memory occurs with repetition and is affected by the intensity of the emotional overtones associated with the memory. This may explain why a phobia can be established in 10 seconds: Fear is an intense emotion.

The hippocampus (1), the cortex of the frontal lobes (2), and the thalami (3) are currently believed to be part of long-term memory storage.

Source: *The Brain, A User's Manual*

In 1970, Eccles wrote:

"I have hopes, too, that we are on the threshold of understanding the basic principles responsible for the laying down of memory traces, which we may envisage as being due to an enduring enhancement of synaptic efficacy with usage. In this way a neuronal pathway that is activated by a particular sensory input will, as a consequence of repeated activation, achieve a kind of stabilization by means of the enhanced synaptic functions of its neuronal linkages. This patterned engram, as it is called, is available for recall in memory when there is an appropriate input into its circuitry."

—*Facing Reality*

How does the engram become patterned, and what is an appropriate input for recall? Neither was known in 1970, but now we know much more about how the learning is patterned.

One amusing anecdote concerning long-term memory is told by William Dement, of Stanford University. In his book, *Some Must Watch While Some Must Sleep*, Dement tells of introducing his course to 800 students this way:

Sellar and Yeatman (*1066 and All That*) firmly state that "history is what you can remember." They claim that the average Englishman can remember only about two dates in history, one of which is almost always the Battle of Hastings. The first time I taught the sleep and dream course, I described this remarkable thesis on history and memory and suggested to the students that if the average Englishman could remember little more than the date 1066, I could hardly expect them to remember the myriad details contained in thousands of publications on sleep and dreams. I would, therefore, I said, undertake a somewhat different pedagogic style and emphasize principles, particularly a few important principles, that I would expect them to remember for the remainder of their lives.

Throughout the ensuing semester I underscored verbally things that the students "should always remember," such as "there are two entirely different kinds of sleep and their names are REM and NREM," "sleeping pills cause insomnia," and so forth. At the end of the semester, well satisfied with myself and my pedagogic philosophy, I gave a multiple-choice examination, with one additional question: "Write one thing from the course that you will surely remember for the rest of your life." Nearly all the students wrote "1066." To this day, I am not sure whether they were telling me something very profound about the educational process or whether their response was just an extremely well-executed put-on.

"Mind, n. — A mysterious form of matter secreted by the brain. Its chief activity consists in the endeavor to ascertain its own nature, the futility of the attempt being due to the fact that it has nothing but itself to know itself with."
  —The Devil's Dictionary

Richard Bandler once said to an audience, in which I sat, "Have you ever thought about all the thoughts you've never had?"

Stimulus-Response (Habit Learning)

Stimulus-response, or habit learning, seems to have fewer components and shorter circuitry than cognitive memory learning, and takes place in a different part of the brain. Stimulus-response is quick and thus appropriate for fast motor responses, such as catching a glass of water before it spills.

The corpus striatum, a complex of structures in the forebrain, may be where stimulus-response learning is coded. The corpus striatum receives projections from the cortex and sends fibers to the parts of the brain that control motor movement.

The striatum is an old part of the brain developmentally, and habit seems to be primitive as well. Sometimes considered part of the basal ganglia, the striatum consists of two structures (one located near the thalamus, the other in the brain stem).

Stimulus-response learning (like seeing your shoestring untied and bending over to tie it) may not have emotions attached. If it does (such as irritation over the need to tie the shoestring now), the entire process is still simpler than cognitive memory learning.

"Is it not true that the most common of our experiences are accepted without any appreciation of their tremendous mystery? . . . There is good reason to believe that spatio-temporal patterns involving tens of millions of . . . cells must be activated before we experience even the simplest sensation."
—Facing Reality

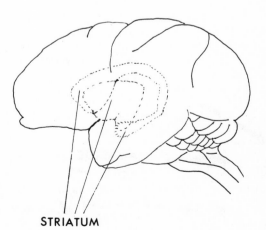

STRIATUM

Cognitive Memory Learning (Stimulus-Response plus Associations)

Cognitive learning is extremely complex in that it moves from the original stimulus to a response, then to associations from the original response. These associations have emotional components with feedback loops to the sensory stimuli. The emotions are coloring the perceptions, and the perceptions are triggering the emotions. Cognitive memory learning seems to go round and round. An example is losing your job and feeling rejected, scared, angry, and concerned about your future. You may go back in time, then forward in time, imagining all sorts of disasters.

Complex learning processes have not yet all been mapped.

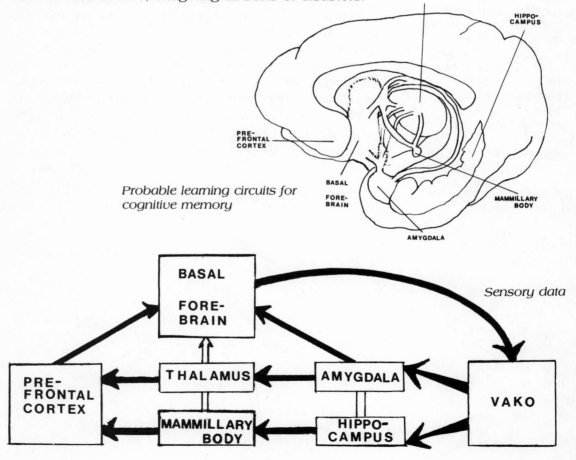

Probable learning circuits for cognitive memory

Cognitive memory has been the focus of new research by brain scientists, among them Mortimer Mishkin, Tim Appenzeller, and Barry Jones.

The amygdala and the hippocampus, located in the subcortical areas of the brain, seem to be important parts of the learning circuit for cognitive memory. By removing both organs from monkeys, Mishkin and Jones were able to create amnesia for learned tasks. The monkeys who lacked an amygdala and a hippocampus could remember a learned task for a minute or so, but no longer.

Related research indicates that the amygdala links emotions with sensory experiences. Why do we store in memory only certain pieces of an experience? Mishkin and Appenzeller considered this issue: "How does the brain single out significant stimuli from the welter of impressions supplied by the senses? If emotions can affect sensory processing in the cortex, they might provide the needed filter, tending to limit attention—and hence learning—to stimuli with emotional significance."

Complex learning with "emotional significance" seems to be a different kind of learning from simple stimulus-response. Complex learning begins with stimulus-response, then goes on to associations. Each response becomes a stimulus for yet another response. These linked responses are the associations culled from different parts of the brain. Complex learning could be portrayed as stimulus-response plus associations.

The limbic system seems to be the relay station that connects our present sensory data to our emotions.

So we seem to learn by means of both *stimulus-response* and *cognitive memory.* When we learn simple habits, both a stimulus and a response are recorded in our brains. Our perception of the stimulus (what we see, hear, touch, taste, and smell) and our response to that perception are closely linked in our brains. When we lay down the more complex cognitive memory learning, we have multiple stimuli plus responses plus whatever associations happen to be activated.

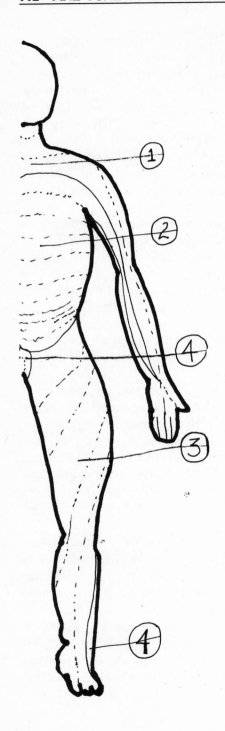

BRAIN/BODY CONNECTIONS

Change Your Body Position—
Change Your Brain

The spinal nerves connect the body to the brain and could be viewed as extensions of the brain.

Different spinal nerves receive and send messages to and from distinct areas of the body surface. These zones are named dermatones.

Cervical nerves serve dermatone area 1.

Thoracic nerves serve dermatone area 2.

Lumbar nerves serve dermatone area 3.

Sacral nerves serve dermatone area 4.

Pain in a body area causes an automatic reflex so that response is immediate. Sexual arousal can be triggered by stimulating 19 separate areas, causing a reflex action along a pathway to the genitals, the spinal column and the brain, and back again.

Dendrites

Some neurons
are almost a
meter long;
some are only a
few millimeters.

AXON

Cell body

Sensory Neuron

The body's com-
munication sys-
tem and brain's
sensory neurons
have many differ-
ent sizes and
shapes. Affer-
ents bring sig-
nals to the
central nervous
system from
elsewhere. Effer-
ents send sig-
nals out.
Interneurons
(brain and spinal
cord) communi-
cate between the
other two types.

ELECTROCHEMICAL CONNECTIONS

The Electrochemical Nature of the Neuron Synapse

The narrow gap between
one neuron and another
is crossed by a chemical
neurotransmitter that triggers an impulse in the
other neuron by making
its covering permeable to
sodium ions. The bul-
bous shape at the end of
the axon is called a syn-
aptic button. The small
sacs fuse with the cover-
ing membrane and
release the neurotransmitter (brain chemical).

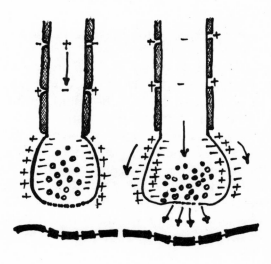

BEHAVIORAL VERSUS COGNITIVE PSYCHOLOGY

Behaviorists and cognitivists have long disagreed about how we learn. Behaviorists focus on stimulus-response, or habit learning, and cognitivists focus on learning that involves knowledge, memory, and expectations. Now it appears that both schools of thought may be right; the brain may learn in more than one way.

Mishkin and Appenzeller offer a way to reconcile the conflicting theories of the behaviorists and the cognitivists: "Behavior could be a blend of automatic responses to stimuli and actions guided by knowledge and expectation."

Behavior could be a blend of **simple learning**—automatic responses to simuli (stimulus-response) and **complex learning**—actions guided by knowledge and expectation (stimulus-response patterns, or stimulus-response plus associations).

Mortimer Mishkin and Tim Appenzeller offer a reconciliation to behaviorists and cognitivists:

"Habits as we define them are reminiscent of the automatic stimulus-response bonds that behaviorist psychologists long ago argued are the basis of all learning. The behaviorist point of view excludes such terms as 'mind,' 'knowledge,' and even 'memory' in its usual sense. It stands in opposition to cognitive psychology which relies on those very concepts to account for much of behavior. The possibility that learning is built on two quite different systems, one of them a source of non-cognitive habits and the other the basis of cognitive memory, offers a way to reconcile the behaviorist and cognitivist schools."

—"The Anatomy of Memory," *Scientific American*, June 1987

A New Theory About Behavioral Change

If Mishkin and Appenzeller's theory is correct about the two types of learning—habit (stimulus-response) and cognitive memory (stimulus-response plus associations)—it may explain some of the mysteries I have observed in the past eight years while teaching the processes of reframing, marqueeing, change history, accessing a resource state, and so forth. The far-reaching behavioral changes I have seen were beyond my ability to explain. Their main drawback may have been their simplicity; people cannot believe deep change is so easy.

However, now that research has uncovered new information about the two different ways the brain learns, new theories are emerging about what may be happening in the advanced change techniques. Perhaps what is happening is a transfer of cognitive memory learning to stimulus-response circuits. This would mean that one's responses to stimuli are quicker, shorter, and more efficient. Or maybe the move is in the other direction—from stimulus-response to simulus-response plus associations. Selected components are exactly what we want in the circuitry—not old emotions that are no longer useful. We may be restructuring our memory act, leaving in our circuits only the responses we want.

One way to explain the powerful changes of reframing, change history, and resource states would be to theorize that these are the result of changing circuits in the brain—streamlining the processes of useful patterns and replacing negative ones. An even more likely explanation is offered by Dr. Issy Katzeff, who theorizes that these processes are cognitive memory and that the cognitive memory process itself is altered by these new techniques. (See his contribution on the next page.)

By the time you finish this book you may have an idea about whether these theories are true. Or perhaps some research scientist will uncover new evidence to illuminate our search.

When people do change, they ask:

"If behavioral change is simple, why have I been depressed for so long?"

"Why have I been afraid of heights as long as I can remember?"

A Physiologist and Brain Researcher Writes of Neurolinguistics and Current Theories on Brain Processes

The anatomy and natural processes of the brain seem to be designed for new cognitive learning. To be specific:

1. *Parallel circuitry* and processing
2. *Multiple representations* of the same information in a single area and in several areas
3. Formation of electrochemical neuronal *patterns* or maps of information
4. Inclusion of *feedback loops*, specifically those involving the limbic system and emotions associated with rewards and punishment
5. *Internal states*, both physiological states and states of mind, which impinge on these feedback loops

It is likely that parallel processing and multiple representations create many neuronal options for producing changed or new patterns. Involvement of the feedback loops and mental states determines whether these new patterns will cause long-term neuronal synaptic changes. If they do, these new patterns will be memorized, or learned.

Since behavior is the external expression of neural patterns in the brain, this implies many options for altering behavior, possibly even rapidly, by altering the processing, sequencing, or emotional-state-dependent feedback loops. Any alteration in the sequence can produce new patterns and new behaviors in response to the same stimuli that formerly produced unwanted, or less than optimal, behaviors.

For a long time it has been known that brain patterns are representational maps of the external world. (See diagrams of homunculus page 149.) At the primary sensory level, there is a point-to-point, though not necessarily proportional, representation of the surface of the body on the surface of the postcentral gyrus of the parietal lobe of the cerebral cortex.

It has been shown that electrical stimulation of any point in the brain map will give rise to specific sensation in that part of the body represented by the point on the postcentral gyrus.

The patterns in the brain that have been set down through cognitive learning also represent mappings of "real" world experiences. Since these patterns are dependent on emotional states, and also on cultures and belief systems, it seems likely that further options for altering people's maps, patterns, and behaviors are possible. Recent research has resulted in pictures of these brain maps, using voltage-sensitive dyes or positron-emission transaxial tomography, and these pictures of the brain maps confirm the parallel processing and multiple representations of the neuronal patterns.

Recent behavioral studies using the techniques described here have produced dramatic changes in behaviors. This analysis has lead to increased understanding of the steps required to enable individuals to produce highly effective fine-tuning of their brains. These steps include the stimulus, the processing, the representations, the emotional feedback loops, and the emotional state. Such fine-tuning has resulted in significant alterations in behavioral responses. (For simplicity we will refer to this process as stimulus-response learning.) These behavioral discoveries are totally compatible with the findings of present neurological research.

If you follow the steps of the resource state in the next chapter and produce your resource state, you will systematically be producing the appropriate sequence to learn and to produce those connections in the neuronal patterns in your brain. It seems that this procedure will enable you to trigger the appropriate brain patterns and behaviors which will be linked, through cognitive learning, to this resource state.

Issy Katzeff, M.D. is Senior Lecturer in physiology, Department of Medical Physiology, Witwatersrand University Medical School, Parktown, South Africa, and consultant to the South Africa Brain Research Institute.

Now let's look at some parts of the brain involved in learning, and consider new research and old mysteries. The brain puzzle has many pieces, and we will not be completing the picture here. However, more pieces are beginning to fit together, and new pictures are emerging.

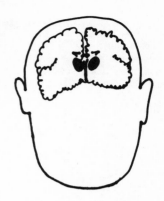

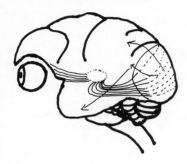

The puzzle of selective attention has fascinated brain scientists for years. Some of the answers seem to lie in the left and right thalami. The left thalamus seems to pay attention to phenomena that suggest words; the right thalamus seems to give its attention to visual images.

Our eyes begin a process that follows two pathways in the outer layer of the brain. First, the "pictures" are processed through the lateral geniculate body, which sends them to the striate cortex for responses to edges and spots of colors. A lower pathway is used for overall shape or color. Finally, the "pictures" go to the inferior temporal cortex for completion. The posteroparietal cortex analyzes a viewed object's position in space.

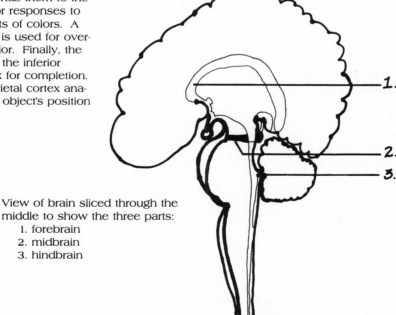

View of brain sliced through the middle to show the three parts:
1. forebrain
2. midbrain
3. hindbrain

THE HORMONAL PUZZLE

Hormones are chemicals that affect our health, brain, and behavior.

Brain is a gland that secretes, among other hormones, opiates— the pain blockers.

Thyroid secretes thyroxin for normal growth.

Heart makes its own hormone— which can reduce blood volume, relax blood vessels, and increase salt disposal.

Pancreas produces and sends out insulin, which regulates carbohydrate (sugar) metabolism.

Adrenals produce epinephrine, which causes acceleration of heart rate; contraction of radial muscle of the iris; rise in systolic blood pressure and pulse rate; an increase in the minute volume of the heart and in respiration. Regulates distribution of water and electrolytes, carbohydrate metabolism, and muscular efficiency.

ACTH and vasopressin (during stress) may stimulate learning and memory.

Pituitary regulates growth. Releases LH and FSH (tells ovaries to produce estrogen). Tells testes to make testosterone; releases oxytocin, for mothering instinct, and prolactin, which stimulates mothers' milk. Also releases adrenocorticotrophic hormone (after a signal from the hypothalamus), which prompts—

Adrenals to produce cortisol, which raises blood sugar levels and speeds up metabolism. (Shy kids have higher levels of cortisol than aggressive kids.)

Ovaries produce estrogen. Progesterone prepares lining of uterus for egg.

Parathyroids provide hormone necessary for calcium metabolism.

In 1970, only 20 hormones were known; now there may be as many as 200.

These old and new puzzle pieces— only part of the known hormone picture— may affect our learning processes.

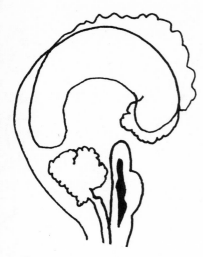

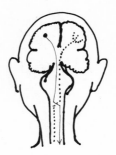

The brain stem carries information from the spinal cord to the cerebral hemispheres. The dotted line indicates sensory signals flowing into the brain, and the straight line shows motor impulses going out to the muscles. Each side of the brain controls movements of and receives information from the opposite side of the body.

The reticular formation located in the center of the brain stem contains a number of nuclei that are part of the reticular activating system. This system also plays an important role in learning.

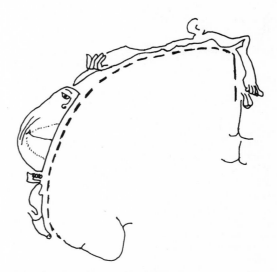

Homunculus—a little man created by the imagination

Representational maps of motor impulses from body areas are located in the precentral gyrus. This homunculus is based on the work of Wilder Penfield.

Representational maps of sensory impulses from body areas are located in the postcentral gyrus, according to Penfield.

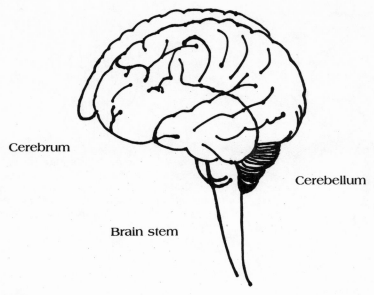

Cerebrum

Cerebellum

Brain stem

Language and the Brain

1. The left frontal lobe of the brain is the location of Broca's area, which controls the production of speech.

2. Behind Broca's area is Wernicke's area which governs the understanding of speech. Wernicke's area is in the left temporal and parietal lobes.

If the links between these two areas are damaged, spontaneous speech creation is hindered, but repetition of speech is still possible.

Writing and the Brain

By electrically stimulating portions of the brain, scientists have been able to ascribe functions to certain areas. Although the area that controls the ability to write varies somewhat from individual to individual, this location is the most common.

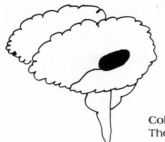

Colors and the Brain

The ability to identify colors seems to be located in the back of the brain near the visual cortex. Certain people, artists in particular, have finer color distinction than others. The ability to see skin color changes can be learned. An important first step in this learning is to believe that subtle colors, not perceived before, do exist. Then the learning occurs rapidly.

Naming and the Brain

Research into language and the brain has yet to explain how we choose our words and how we sequence these words in a meaningful manner. How we attach certain meanings to certain perceptions and then select our words to reflect these perceptions are also still unexplained. When Adam and Eve named the animals in the Garden of Eden, they may have stored the names in this area.

Reading and the Brain

Language areas vary somewhat from person to person. The above darkened area is approximately the area that allows us to read Shakespeare, newspapers, and billboards.

Some people understand what they read by repeating the words; others can bypass this step by turning the words into pictures, sounds, or feelings.

PAVLOV RINGS A BELL

In 1901, Ivan Pavlov demonstrated not only that responses are linked to stimuli but that new responses can be *learned*. When Pavlov rang a bell and the dogs salivated, he demonstrated the stimulus-response pattern that the dogs had learned: bell-saliva. The natural stimulus-response pattern is food-saliva. Pavlov took a natural physical mechanism—stimulus-response—and hooked up an "unnatural" stimulus. Because dogs cannot eat sounds or bells, salivating at a bell was an unnatural response.

When we think, we use similar stimulus-response connections in our brain patterns. The processes we go through—the chemical and electrical changes that take place—determine which words come out of our mouth and which facial expressions, gestures, and body postures we use to reinforce our meaning.

Each instance of brain activity has its own specific pattern, with corresponding electrical and chemical components. Those patterns, which are wavelike and of measurable duration, are our thoughts.

Nerve cells, called *neurons*, form the network on which thought patterns occur. We have billions of these nerve cells, and we use them to perceive and respond to stimuli—to categorize, to name, and to decide on actions. "In a single human brain the number of possible interconnections between these cells *is greater than the number of atoms in the universe,*" write Robert Ornstein and Richard Thompson. It is these interconnections that allow us to code our perceptions, to think, and then to speak. Our thoughts are patterns set up by these nerve cells and their interconnections, and our language is the result of these patterns. The words we learn and use are coded into these patterns in our brains.

When we learn, it appears that both a stimulus and a response are recorded in our brains. Our perceptions of the stimulus (what we see, hear, touch, taste, and smell) and our response to those perceptions (fear, pleasure, pain) are linked in our brains. The perception recorded by the original stimulus may

Not all stimuli are recorded at the perceptual level. Our perceptions of the stimuli are probably recorded in the form of patterns.

Stimulus—a smell, taste, picture, sound, touch, or sensation that evokes a specific brain pattern

Response—the habitual brain pattern elicited by an immediate perception or a memory of certain perceptions

become the beginning of a pattern, even if the entire original stimulus is not coded as memory.

UNNATURAL HOOKUPS

Most of us have some unnatural responses that have been hooked accidentally to stimuli. A stimulus-response pattern is so easy to set up that unlikely hookups are common. For example, many of us have had the experience of being called on to give an answer in class and not being able to do so, perhaps because we had not done the homework, were uncomfortable about making a presentation, or were not sure whether we understood the material. Years later, when called on suddenly in a business meeting, we may have the same response. With boss and colleagues looking on, we suddenly go blank, this time when we know the information very well. This is an unnatural hookup; going blank when called on is not a useful response.

Some unnatural hookups are useful, and some are not. You can learn how to recognize and improve your automatic responses to stimuli—automatic responses that are often the result of unnatural hookups that occurred in your brain during your development. If you go blank when your boss calls on you in a meeting, you will discover how to change that response. If you have a fear of disaster hooked to the ring of the telephone late at night or to the sight of a telegram, you will discover how to change that response.

Cognitive learning uses more complex circuitry than habit learning.

Current knowledge and theories about how the brain works are far too complex to be covered in this book, and with simplification comes the possibility of error. The amazing functions of the human brain cannot be accurately reduced to stimulus-response. And, for many people, the phrase "stimulus-response" has negative mechanistic overtones. In this book, I want to emphasize the choice that seems to be inherent in brain patterns. The term "stimulus-response pattern" is used here in a broader sense, to refer to the basic neurological processes of learning—the electrochemical tapestry.

You are encouraged to view the brain as a constantly changing tapestry, with choice as a strand to be woven in at some learning points. With increased awareness of your own stimulus-response patterns comes even greater choice.

Can you think of some automatic responses you have to stimuli? For example, how do you feel when you are driving and you see a police car with blinking red lights in your rearview mirror? When your boss appears at your office door, do you straighten up and look serious? Do you have to stifle the urge to salute when you see a military uniform?

If you are like most of us, stimulus-response patterns run across the brain so quickly that you are not aware they are "unnatural"—that is, they have been set up accidentally or by an unplanned linkage between two separate and unrelated events. You do not *have* to straighten up and breathe more quickly when your boss appears, but if you respond this way automatically, easily, and effortlessly, you are exhibiting a stimulus-response pattern. It might be more useful to smile, frown, or pull out a file. You will never know until you break the old pattern.

September-Register!

A powerful stimulus-response pattern can run for years without your even being aware of it. I collected a B.A., an M.A., worked on another M.A., worked on a Ph.D., and then completed another Ph.D. before I discovered I had a patterned response to the month of September.

The basic mechanism of my stimulus-response was like the one Pavlov installed in his dogs. In my case it was not September-salivate; it was September-register—for almost anything. The subject matter did not matter so long as I was signing up to learn something.

Finally, I got tired of playing student. The September after I realized that, I did not register for any courses. I was very uncomfortable all month, feeling that something was wrong. I finally realized that the source of my discomfort was my not being in school—learning. But I was learning; I was learning something important about my father, stimulus-response plus associations, and me. By staying with the discomfort, I was able to sort it out.

My father had felt frustrated all his life because he had not spent more time in school. Before I was 5 years old, he had taught me to go to school—forever. He had forgotten to add the qualification "as long as appropriate." So when I refused to let my routine but unnatural pattern sequence of September-register run, I experienced a strong negative feeling. Because the stimulus-response plus associations had begun with my father, all the fears of disobeying this omnipotent figure rose up. My father's implanted pattern had worked every year for 35 years. It is somewhat surprising that I was able to interrupt such a firmly entrenched pattern because each time a stimulus-response plus associations runs, it is more likely to run again.

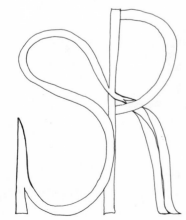

ENGRAMS

Earlier in this chapter we referred to an "engram." J. C. Eccles used this term to describe a well-learned pattern of response. In *Facing Reality*, Eccles states, "A neuronal pathway that is activated by a particular sensory input will, as a consequence of repeated activation, achieve a kind of stabilization. . . . This patterned engram, as it is called, is available for recall in memory when there is an appropriate input into its circuitry." Thus, a well-learned pattern—called an engram—is more likely to run than a new, weak pattern. And when a habit or cognitive memory has stabilized—has become a pattern—the same series of responses always follows a particular stimulus.

A really well-laid-down engram—a stabilized pattern— gives you no choice. It runs quickly, automatically, and effortlessly. This is very useful if the response is how you want to behave or think, such as applying the brake when you see a red light. But if the response is something you do not want—such as overeating, smoking, or enrolling in classes—you need to recognize the pattern and make some changes. Most people who are doing something that they do not want to do are on an automatic pattern track. They simply have no choice.

Synaptic juncture

The Electrochemical Nature of the Neuron Synapse

The narrow gap between one neuron and another is crossed by a chemical neurotransmitter that triggers an impulse in the other neuron.

Change your chemicals.
Change your brain patterns.
Change your behavior.

An engram's automatic pattern depends on chemicals to begin the electrical impulses that propagate the thought across the axons and dendrites of the nerve cell. Ornstein and Thompson write, "Neurons talk to each other by releasing certain chemical molecules, the chemical messengers, or neurotransmitters, at the synapses. . . . When these molecules reach the target-cell membrane, the postsynaptic membrane, they attach to chemical receptor molecules that are a part of the postsynaptic membrane." The method the messengers use to find the right receptor is much like using a key that fits only a certain lock. Thoughts connect to other specific thoughts, or not. The associations the word "home" has for you—security, comfort, pleasure, or whatever—are set up by electrical and chemical connections inside your head.

Edward de Bono's Six Ways to Think:
1. *Facts, figures, and objective information*
2. *Emotions and feeling*
3. *Logical negative thoughts*
4. *Positive constructive thoughts*
5. *Creativity and new ideas (innovation)*
6. *Control of thinking processes and steps*

At one time it was thought that only three or four different chemical messenger molecules exist. Now researchers estimate that hundreds are present in thought transmission. These chemicals cause electrical responses at the synaptic clefts and inside the axons so that electrical activity carries the pattern across the brain. Change your chemicals; change your brain patterns; change your behavior. You do not have to live with behavior patterns that are no longer working to get you what you want. You can set up new patterns to replace the old ones.

In *Eye to Eye: The Quest for the New Paradigm,* Ken Wilber presents a convincing case for three levels of knowing:

> sensory
> mental
> spiritual

Our brains have the basic hardware for all three types of knowing.

Becoming Aware of Patterns

If you do not want a pattern to run automatically, you have to interrupt it with choice. First, you have to become aware that a stimulus-response or a cognitive memory pattern is at work. Take a few minutes and think of several of your well-learned brain patterns or engrams. Can you pick out three you like and three you dislike? To get you started, here are six personal engrams I like:

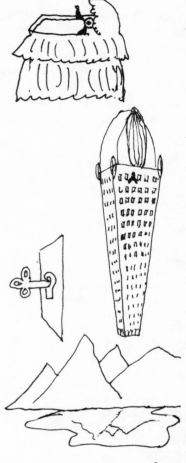

STIMULUS	RESPONSE PATTERN
Sound of my baby crying in the middle of the night	Without being wide awake, I hop out of bed and go check on her.
A fire alarm in a hotel at night	I leap out of bed and look out the window (not always pleasant but useful for survival).
The sight of my dogs	I feel secure.
My husband's key in the lock at night	I feel good.
A beautiful view	I long for my paints.
The sight of my six children after an absence	I get a lump in my throat. I look at my children and am aware of how beautiful they are. I want to touch each of them.

These responses run so quickly and so consistently that I know I have no choice in having them. If I am in disagreement with my husband, I remember the disagreement *after* the good feeling at the sound of the key. At that point I have a choice: Shall I focus on the disagreeable feeling or the good feeling? Now here are some examples of personal engrams I dislike:

STIMULUS	RESPONSE PATTERN
Overdraft notice from the bank	Tight stomach
Dogs barking in the night	Wide awake; adrenaline rush (potentially useful for survival, but irritating because it is usually a false alarm)
IRS return address on a registered letter	Tight stomach, tense shoulders, stiff neck
Harsh criticism of my teaching style	Tight stomach
Even a gentle putdown from one of my kids	Tears and a tight throat
The words "I have some bad news" on a long distance call	Bone-chilling fear

I dislike the no-choice aspect of these responses, although in many cases the response and its association may be appropriate. Even so, I would like to have a choice. I end up with a tight stomach and stiff neck muscles more often than I would like. But I know that when a response bothers me enough, I can change it—just as I changed my September-register pattern.

Paradigm of the Organism?

One of the more controversial theories on memory and learning is Rupert Sheldrake's hypothesis of formative causation, which proposes that organisms are shaped by "morpho-genetic fields associated with previous similar systems." Through a process Sheldrake calls "morphic resonance," these fields of "past systems become *present* to any subsequent similar system; the structures of past systems affect subsequent similar systems by a cumulative influence which acts across both space *and time*." Thus, if laboratory rats learn a task in London, their French cousins (assuming breeding and environmental conditions are parallel) will learn the same task more quickly, as will the next generation of rats.

Sheldrake applies this concept to human learning, as well. "The hypothesis of formative causation provides an alternative interpretation, in the light of which the persistence of learned habits in spite of damage to the brain is far less puzzling: the habits depend on motor fields which are not stored within the brain at all, but are given directly from its past states by morphic resonance."

In the following chapters you will learn how to change many of the responses and associations you do not like and how to set up a new response or a new pattern of responses to a stimulus. By linking specific responses to specific stimuli, you can create any mental state you desire.

Right now think of a goal or an outcome you want. Then think of the best mental state you could be in to achieve it. Can you see how it would be extraordinarily useful to create the optimum mental state in yourself before you make a presentation of a new idea, close a sale, or do anything that requires you to be at your best? We call that optimum state a *resource state*, or a *state of excellence*. When you are in a state of excellence, your mental resources—learned from past experience—are easily accessible for immediate use. By using the stimulus-response and cognitive learning mechanisms by which your brain learns, you can trigger that resource state whenever you wish.

*The hippocampus, the
amygdala, and the state of
excellence*

Our personalities may result from
accidental stimulus-response patterns.

9
The Resource State

Consider for a moment the possibility that some facets of your unique personality are the result of accidental stimulus-response patterns established by random experiences. These patterns run so fast that you accept your personality as a given, without considering the random nature of some, if not all of the patterns responsible for its development. Personality traits, such as frugality, extravagance, neatness, punctuality, tardiness, shyness, and aggressiveness, may be the result of long-forgotten early experiences.

Once you become aware of your patterns, you can keep the ones that work toward making you happy, content, exhilarated, peaceful, or whatever state you desire. You can also change patterns that lead to other, less satisfactory internal states.

When you learn how to control your stimulus-response mechanisms, you can choose to respond in a way that is emotionally and psychologically optimal for you. This type of response gives you access to all the resources you have acquired during your life. By altering your learning mechanisms, you can create this *resource state* any time you wish. You simply need to learn how to set up a new stimulus-response or a new response pattern to an old stimulus. Both processes are similar.

Stimulus-response patterns (stimulus-response plus associations)—cognitive learning

THE BRAIN AS A MARQUEE

J. C. Eccles has a visual metaphor for how perceptions and thoughts cross the brain and link up into sequences. Eccles compares the brain to a theater marquee, which has an extensive network of lights. Thoughts move across the brain in an ever-changing pattern, analogous to the way marquee lights are illuminated to create words. The same lightbulbs, used in various patterns, spell many different words. Lights are switched on for some words and switched off for others.

You can write whatever coming attractions you want on your theater marquee.

The nerve cells, or neurons, in the brain work the same way: Some are activated to transmit certain thoughts while others remain "dark." When we switch on a certain pattern of nerve cells to set up a response to a stimulus, our brain acts like a theater marquee. Just as the theater marquee has the potential for spelling out any name, our brain has the potential of lighting up with any response we have ever had or imagined. Once we have learned a response pattern—such as pleasure or confidence—we can light up that same response again. The tricky part is knowing how and when to set up the response pattern you want.

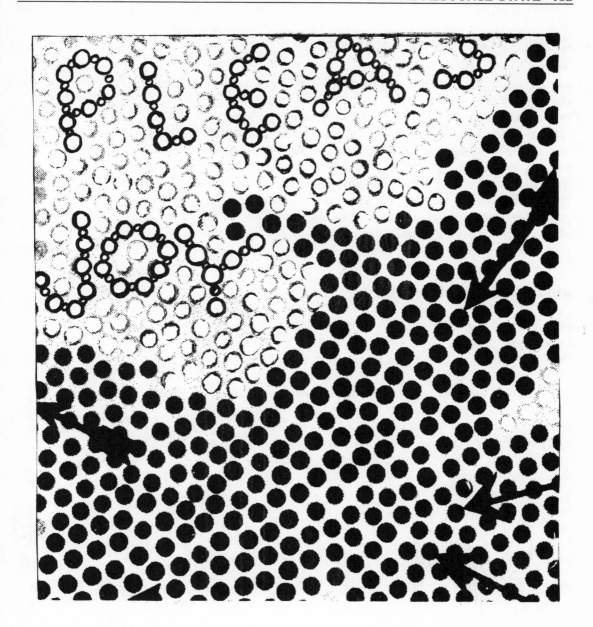

Marquee—a metaphor for thoughts lighting up parts of the brain.
Pleasure and joy are useful engrams with which to light up your marquee.

CUE-KEY: A PLANNED STIMULUS

To set up a resource state, we first need a planned stimulus. This can be visual, auditory, kinesthetic, olfactory, or gustatory—or any combination of these. I call a planned stimulus a *cue-key*, as a reminder that all our senses are available as stimuli. "Cue," a word or signal to performers, is good for auditories and visuals because it prompts them to recall something they know. "Key" is good for kinesthetics, to remind them that their resources can be unlocked and placed within their grasp. A key is also easy for visuals to picture and for auditories to hear as it unlocks their resources.

Cue-key—a new stimulus or an old stimulus that will be linked to a new response pattern

RESOURCE STATE: A PLANNED RESPONSE

Like a stimulus, a response can be visual, auditory, kinesthetic, olfactory, and/or gustatory. Moreover, it does not have to involve the same senses as the stimulus. The best planned response to a stimulus would be the best response imaginable—one that draws on all our resources. I call this planned response a state of excellence, or a resource state. In this chapter you will learn how to create a resource state so that your best response to a situation will be available any time you wish.

Cell types found in the cerebellum. Nature shows infinite variety in the designs of its communication components

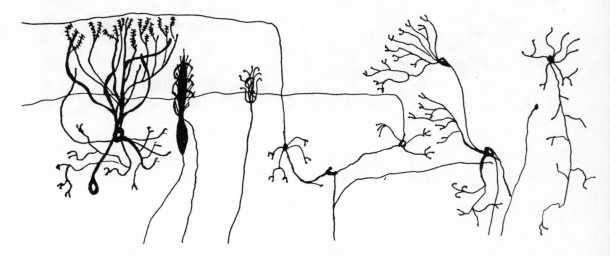

Backtrack on Stimulus-Response Patterns

Engram—a planned or well-learned stimulus-response pattern

Before we look at the exact steps for creating a resource state, let's review what you know about stimulus-response patterns.

- The stimulus-response process is a basic mechanism of the brain.
- A stimulus-response that has become stabilized—an engram—is a learned pattern that operates without choice.
- A stimulus-response pattern activates electrical and chemical changes in the brain.
- Until now, many of your stimulus-response patterns have been set up accidentally.
- You will find it useful to know how to set up a stimulus-response pattern deliberately.

**STIMULUS-RESPONSE
PATTERN**

Stimulus
  Processing
  Representations
  Electrochemical
    patterns
  Emotional feedback
    loops
  Emotional states

The process condensed

Responses

CREATING A RESOURCE STATE

The first step in setting up a planned response of excellence—a resource state—is to recall when you did something extraordinarily well. Think back to a time when your performance was exceptional, when you surprised yourself with your own ability. It might have been the time you hit the tennis ball perfectly, made a great presentation, cooked a terrific meal, got an A on your paper, or negotiated a very successful contract. Pick one specific instance of accomplishment that really satisfied you, not a category.

Most people with whom I have worked can think of one instance in which they really excelled, and many can think of doing something so well that they later wondered how they had done it. The whole thing went so smoothly that they surprised themselves. If you can recall one of those extraordinary performances in your own life, use it in this exercise.

Resource state—a new response pattern or an old response linked to a new stimulus

If you cannot think of an example right now, do not be concerned. In the next chapter I give you additional approaches and ideas to help you create a resource state. Read through the steps here first so you will understand the process.

See, Hear, Feel the Experience

When you have selected your experience, intensify the memory:

- What did you *see* when you were accomplishing this extraordinary feat?
- What did you *hear*?
- What did you *feel*?

Be sure to actually take a few minutes to resee, rehear, and refeel what you perceived that other time. In order for the process to work, you need to re-create the experience. If you can, assume the same body posture you had when your extraordinary event took place.

When you see the memory in your mind's eye, be sure you are *in* your own body, looking *out* at the world through your own eyes, hearing the sounds through your own ears—using all your senses to re-create and be inside the experience.

If your memory has been stored in a dissociated state, this process will not work. A dissociated state is one in which you are observing yourself from some other position in space—seeing yourself from another point of view. Do not dissociate while setting up your resource state. Look out at the world through your own eyes to recall the feeling parts of your memory. Then actually feel the excitement, the confidence, the satisfaction. These feeling components are essential for creating a state of excellence.

By focusing on the sensory input—the sights, sounds, and feelings—you received at the moment of extraordinary accomplishment, you activate the same electrical and chemical patterns in your brain that

Dissociated State

A *dissociated state* is one in which you imagine you see or hear yourself from another position— outside your own body—or when your feelings are projected from a place outside your body. In a dissociated state, you are often unaware of your feelings.

Many people store memories in a dissociated state—recording the scenes as if viewing them from a point on the ceiling. This can be useful in some situations, but not when setting up a resource state.

were present at the time of the event. These patterns of success—these responses—are what you want to be able to call up whenever you wish.

When you have re-created the event in your memory, you have accessed your resource state. Now you need a planned stimulus—a cue-key—to evoke that response any time you wish.

Imagine a Circle

A
good visual stimulus to
use to create a resource state is
an imaginary circle into which you can
step. The circle will be your cue-key, returning you immediately to a time of extraordinary
accomplishment. It is a good idea to have a code
word, as well as a visual stimulus, to prompt your
response. Then you will have both a picture and a
sound, so you will be using two senses to recall—or
cue-key—the response you want. You do not have to
say the code word out loud; you can say it to yourself. You do not have to draw a circle either, although I sometimes do this for clients who need
to see the circle in order for it to be "real." If
you have difficulty imagining a circle,
by all means get a piece of chalk
and draw one on the floor or
carpet.

Setting Up Your Resource State

When you have your experience, your circle, and your code word, you are ready to create your resource state. Here is the sequence:

1. Picture a time when you did something very well.
   - What do you see?
   - What do you hear?
   - What do you feel?

2. As soon as the images, sounds, and feelings are clear, imagine a circle on the floor. Give the circle a color.

3. Take a deep breath, and step into the circle.

4. Stand inside the circle, and intensify the memory of the extraordinary event.

5. Enjoy the feeling of confidence that is a natural part of doing something well and knowing it.

Now go through the sequence again, adding your code word.

1. Picture a time of resourcefulness.

2. See a colored circle.

3. Say your code word.

4. Step into the circle.

5. Intensify the feeling.

6. Stay in the circle for as long as you clearly experience the resource state.

Take the time now to to go through these steps two more times. This will set up the pattern so that you can easily access your resource state any time you wish.

If you wish to check out the effectiveness of your resource state, try this with a friend.

Tasks of the Friend

Do not stay in a low resource state for more than 20 seconds. Move into your resource circle quickly.

1. Direct the person who is checking his/her resource state to recall a state of low resourcefulness (a stuck state). Notice the signs of this state.
2. Direct him/her to dissociate from the stuck state by changing to a resource state: (a) recalling his/her positive code word, (b) seeing the imaginary circle and remembering its color, and (c) physically stepping into the imaginary circle.
3. Be sure that the person working on the resource state has all the external signs of resourcefulness by the time s/he enters the circle.
4. Make sure s/he regains the resource state and then intensifies the feeling inside the circle. If not, repeat the resource state process until s/he does have a firmly established internal state of confidence.

Breathe!

The deep breath is essential in creating a resource state. I have observed many people set up resource states, and when they reach their desired state, they begin to take long, easy breaths.

Oxygen is essential if human beings are to function at their best. One of the ways we limit our behaviors and our thinking processes is by becoming tense—hunching our shoulders, constricting our chests, and cutting down on our oxygen supply. When we are taking short, tight breaths, our minds and bodies do not get enough oxygen to function at peak performance. It may be that we physically restrict the amount of incoming air by such a posture, or we may have a pattern of failure that we trigger by short breaths.

Any time you are in a "tight" situation, the best thing you can do for yourself is take a deep breath. That alone may trigger your resource state.

Now that you know how to change a stuck state to a resource state quickly, this ability may generalize.

A Circle in Action

Let me tell you how one of my students used his resource state to keep him from being his own worst enemy in business negotiations. Bill grew up in a section of Brooklyn where street gangs were a way of life. He was in his late teens before he realized there were worlds in which you did not have to be ready to fight for your survival each day.

Smart and quick, Bill found he could survive in these other worlds and even make money over and above what he needed for rent. He gravitated toward jobs with glamorous extras, such as hotel promotion. As a promoter, he could lunch in restaurants with 20-page menus and put the bill on his expense account. He was not taking much money home, but he was living a life out of a slick magazine. After a wife or two had left him pretty well stripped of money and self-esteem, he started over to regain both for himself.

Three questions Bill hated at parties:

Where do you work?
Where do you live?
What do you drive?

Bill had an irresistible wit and a lively twinkle in his snapping black eyes. He liked being honest and straight—he had his own integrity. He came to counseling because he had become expert in real estate investments, but he sometimes sabotaged himself at the close.

In his words, "We'll be sitting there, this guy with his pen clutched in his hand ready to sign, and my internal voices will begin. Next thing I know, I say something that will make him put down the pen and walk away." He paused, then continued, "I want to stop that. I get so anxious not to do the wrong thing that I do the wrong thing."

We were sitting facing each other in my office. I said, "First, we'll turn down your internal tapes. Then a resource state would be the best bet so that you will respond appropriately."

"What's a resource state?" He perched, rather than sat, in his chair. He looked as if he might get up and run at any moment.

My voice was calm and steady as I said, "An internal state that computes all the odds and comes up with the appropriate behavior for the situation in view of your outcome."

"How do I get this infernal state?" he asked, without a lot of interest. He kept looking around the room, not at me.

"Not 'infernal state'—internal state. A mental state, an attitude, a resource state. Let's do it, and then we'll see if it will do what you want."

I taught Bill how to turn down his internal audiotapes and then offered to show him how to set up his resource state. He was now becoming interested.

"Now?" He looked nervously around the room as if looking for an exit.

"Yes, now."

"Will it hurt?"

"Usually not. But let's see. Go back to one of the real estate deals that closed—a big one, one in which you were pleased with your performance." He closed his eyes, his chin raised, his shoulders went back. I continued, "That's the one. Now listen to the voices at the close. Now recall the feeling. Yes, that's the feeling you want." I waited three or four minutes then said, "Come back to the present here and now when you are ready." He immediately opened his eyes.

I continued, "OK, you can set up a resource state easily. Let's do it."

"That was just getting ready?" Surprise was in his voice.

"Yes. Let's stand up to do this. Can you imagine a circle on the floor in front of you?"

"Flat or floating?"

"It doesn't matter—whichever you prefer."

"Floating." He was getting into the game.

"What color is it?" I asked.

He opened his eyes. "I have to give it a color?"

"Well, you don't have to, but it helps."

"Helps what?"

"Helps the clarity of the visualization."

Pause. His eyes closed once more. "OK, it's red." He was amused that he had found a color.

"Now go back to the close of the real estate deal. What do you see?" I paused as his chin came up, his shoulders straightened, his breathing deepened. "What do you hear?" I paused a full minute. I could see a barely perceptible movement of his eyes behind his lids. As it slowed, I asked, "Now—can you recall the feeling?"

His breathing paused, then resumed even deeper in his abdomen. I continued, "Now take a deep breath and step into the circle." I took Bill's arm and sort of nudged him forward. He was so deep in his memory that he did not respond at once. Slowly he put one foot forward, then brought the other foot forward and stood swaying slightly back and forth in the circle. After three minutes, I asked him to return from his memory.

We then went through the process again so he could add the word that is his auditory cue-key for the state of excellence. Then I moved him to the other side of his circle so he was facing in the opposite direction as before—to give him a different visual orientation. I asked him if he could remember one of the times when his behavior had sabotaged a real estate closure. He nodded "yes" as his breathing became shallow, his face paled, and a small muscle in his clenched jaw jumped slightly, its pulsation matching his breathing.

"OK, that's enough of the negative experience," I said, moving closer and taking his elbow lightly. "Now imagine your red circle, see your excellence pictures, hear the sounds, take a deep breath, say your code word, and step into the circle."

He followed my instructions to the letter, and I watched carefully to be sure we were in sync. I left him in his circle of excellence for a minute or so; then I brought his attention back to the room and the present.

Recall a time when you did something well. What did you see?
hear?
feel?

Bill opened his eyes wide, "What a trip!"

"What happened?"

"It was like a tennis game. First the negative picture would flash, and I'd see the client putting down his pen; then the positive picture would flash, and I'd see this other guy's signature on a $2 million contract, then back and forth until finally the positive picture won the game."

"How do you feel now?"

"On top of the world. But how do I do this without you?"

"By taking a deep breath and saying your code word. Try it now."

His eyes closed, and his breath grew deeper again. Then he asked, "Can I do it with my eyes open?"

"I don't know. Try it. You'll look funny closing your eyes every time a client picks up a pen to sign a contract."

He opened his eyes very wide, into an exaggerated oval shape, and said, "Success." He waited a moment, took a breath, and whispered, "Yes, it does work—the word works all by itself. And now it's a one-sided tennis game. I get only the positive pictures."

"Good. I think we're finished."

Within a few weeks Bill was one of the principals of the biggest real estate swap in history. Thirty or so people all swapped property at one time, and his clients were key to the entire arrangement. He called me and said, "I use the resource state every day. And I keep thinking about what you said, 'Know what you want, find out what they want, and close.' "

"No, I didn't say that. I didn't say 'close,' I said 'dovetail.' "

"Same thing."

"If you're thinking of the other person's interests, it's the same thing."

"It's the only way to stay in business in my business," he said.

"Great! And congratulations."

Bill's passion is tennis, and his dream is to inherit a million and play tennis all day. He may make his own million now that he is beginning to know himself and can focus with less internal conflict.

A few months later Bill made, maybe not quite a million, but a lot of money on another spectacular business deal. In explaining how this happened, he said he finally came to believe that he deserved to make money, and so he did.

A Flower-Circle

Rosemary's problem was not money, but martyrdom. She was overweight and had a whiny voice that eclipsed her positive characteristics. An overblown rose with the petals turning under and bruised in spots where people had pressed too hard, she was determined to move up in the corporation or leave her job.

Rosemary came to our meeting in a navy blue wool gabardine suit with a white blouse. The mandatory silk tie of navy, sky blue, and rose was tied in a simple bow. Her navy shoes were corporation regulation as well. She had read *Dress for Success* and taken it seriously.

Rosemary ran a busy regional office for a large corporation. She had begun as a typist and was now regional vice president, but with low wages and long hours. She had been effacing herself for the good of the organization for 12 years and was ready to change her behavior. She had even decided to resign her position and look for another job unless the corporation began to reward her in more concrete ways. Her annual cost-of-living raises were no longer reward enough. She had watched less competent individuals move up the corporate ladder again and again, while she got bigger titles but little else.

Rosemary's colleagues and subordinates resented her changing behavior. She had begun by requesting them to work overtime instead of handling all the extra work herself. They were complying, but with resentment. She thought she might have to change some personnel.

Rosemary also informed her manager that a new directive was not applicable to her office and would cost more to implement than it would produce. After years of having her follow directives loyally, he did not know whether to fire her or congratulate her. He thought she was right, but her refusal put him in a bind.

Rosemary came to me to learn how to stiffen her backbone. We decided to set up a resource state that she could move in and out of all day during her transition.

This morning, Rosemary stood inside a large flower in my carpet. The flower was a rosy color and roughly circular in shape. She had trouble visualizing, so she needed a real circle for her circle of excellence. She was looking down at the flower-circle as she asked, "Are you sure this will work?"

"No," I replied. "Where behaviors, especially new behaviors, are concerned, I'm never sure of anything. But it takes only ten minutes or so, and it is certainly worth a try."

She looked reluctant, her feet moving uneasily inside the rosy flower. I was standing next to her on the beige background of the carpet, and I asked her to step outside the circular flower.

"Why?" she asked.

"Because I want you inside the circle, the flower, only when you are in your state of excellence."

"OK." She moved out of the flower and said, "I don't know if I'll be able to do this. I'm not good at imagining things."

"I know," I said. "You've already told me that."

RETAIN STATE of EXCELLENCE WHILE IN CIRCLE

"Oh, yes," she replied. "But most people do not listen, and I have to tell them twice. You listen. It's disconcerting."

"Can you remember a time when you were pleased with your own performance?" I asked.

No response.

I continued, "You have your entire life to choose from—any age. Go back as far as you want. Select a time when you felt good about yourself."

No response. I waited.

She finally answered, "Well, I felt sort of good when my boss flew into town just to tell me I'd been made a vice president—the first woman vice president in our corporation. However, I knew it was not going to make much difference in my job. There are 200 regional vice presidents." Rosemary's voice lost energy and trailed off.

"Can you remember when he first told you about your new title?"

"Yes." More energy, resonance, could be heard in her voice.

"Just remember him telling you. Stop the movie before the 'however' and 'yes, buts' begin." My voice was more crisp and directive.

"Oh, OK, but it's a short movie."

You can edit your own movie memories.

"Run it over and over. Make the colors brighter."

"It's in grey and white. No colors."

"Can you give it colors?"

Pause. "Well, they are kind of pale."

"Can you increase their intensity?"

"Just a little."

"Can you hear his voice telling you that you are a vice president?"

"He handed me a list of the new appointees."

"Did he say anything?"

"Oh, I'd forgotten. Yes, he said 'congratulations.' "

As Rosemary said "congratulations," she stopped breathing.

"Take a deep breath, and hear him say 'congratulations' again—and again and again. Now how do you feel?"

"I can really hear his voice now. I do not think I really concentrated on his voice at the time, but I must have heard it because I can hear it now." As she said this, Rosemary turned a bright pink.

"OK, now hold on to that feeling and step into the flower."

Once she had stepped forward, I said, "Now intensify the feeling as you hear 'congratulations!' Do it again. And again."

Rosemary's chin raised, her face softened. She looked ten years younger but more authoritative somehow. After a minute, she opened her eyes and said, "What a lovely feeling."

"Step out of the circle. Save the circle for that feeling. Now I want you to find a word for your state of excellence."

"Oh, 'congratulations' is the word."

"Of course." I continued to direct her with these words: "Now go back to the moment your boss handed you the list of newly appointed vice presidents; then read your name on the list; then hear him say. . . ."

Rosemary interrupted, "Well, actually we talked over some things before he said. . . ."

I broke in quickly, "Skip that part of your memory. Just jump from seeing your name on the list to hearing your boss say 'congratulations!' As she reached the sound portion of her movie, my hand on her elbow pushed her forward into the flower-circle. Her pink color came up again, her breath shifted to deep in her abdomen, and her chin came up again. This time I left her in the circle for a good three minutes.

When she was finished with her memory, we sat down to talk over her experience, and she asked, "What will happen if I need to use this five or six times a day?"

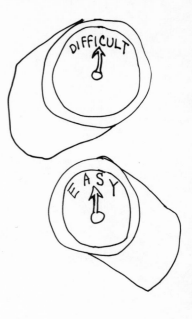

"I'm not sure. Different people have different experiences with their resource states. In my case, it became easier to remember to use it."

"That will be hard . . . to remember to use it."

"Only if you think it will be hard." She sort of jerked and looked at me intensely.

Then she said, "Oh, you mean, it *could* be *easy* to remember."

"If you think it will be easy, it will be easy. If you think it will be difficult, it will be difficult. At least, that's my own experience," I said, as I looked out the window at the white fluffs in a blue sky.

"I hear you. I don't know that I agree with you." Her voice hardened slightly.

I continued, "There are no guarantees. You are beginning to change a set of behaviors you've used for 34 years. These behaviors have cut deep grooves in your brain; they are patterns that are well laid down. The synapses between your neurons are well stabilized. To change deep-seated behaviors is no small task. You will have to interrupt well-established patterns. Are you sure you want to do this?"

"Oh, yes."

"Then take each behavior, interrupt the pattern, and try a new response. Begin with one pattern an hour. Let's say twelve a day. That's a lot. But if you are serious, and I can see you are, you can change twelve old responses a day."

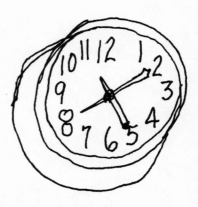

"How about if we decide now which twelve old responses I will change on the first day." I nodded "yes," and she continued, "Here's the first. Three of my employees often arrive late for work. I never say anything about it because it's only 15 minutes or so, and I dislike confrontations." Pause. "I will confront them about this if they are late."

"That's one, or maybe that's three."

"My boss insists that I interrupt whatever I'm doing if he calls. I want to be able to call him back if the interruption is not convenient for me."

"Can you discuss this with him?"

"Yes."

"That's two, or five."

"I want a full hour for lunch. I have a full hour only every two weeks."

"Can you set that up?"

"Yes."

"That's three, or six."

"I want to tell Cindy that three personal phone calls a day are enough."

"Can you do that?"

"Yes."

"That will be four, or seven."

The result of all this planning was that Rosemary took control of her office in a way that improved production, communication, and her self-image. She learned to establish group outcomes and use group synergy instead of taking all the responsibility on herself.

Within three months she had changed some personnel, set up a weekly information exchange with her staff, engaged them in her outcomes, and received a 25 percent raise in salary. She had effaced herself and lived for her work for so many years that her co-workers resented the worm turning, but turning it was.

The worm turning

It is exciting to see a light turn on—as it did when Rosemary became aware that she could own the way she already is and feel good about it. A tree does not apologize for sending its roots down for the water and minerals it needs to grow. As Rosemary accepts herself, positive changes will follow.

Change your state.
Change your chemicals.
Change your reality.

GENERALIZE THE RESPONSE

Once you have learned how to set up a resource state, as Bill and Rosemary did, *use this skill*. The more you use it, the more automatic it will become. The more automatic the response, the more generalized it will become. It will be triggered by other stimuli.

When we learn, generalization helps us transfer what we learned in one situation to other, similar situations. When generalization occurs, we can relate similar events to similar meanings. For example, when we learn how one door key works, we can generalize that knowledge to other doors and other keys.

The positive aspects of a planned stimulus-response pattern naturally tend to generalize. This means that if you decide to use your resource state each time your boss raises his/her voice, you may find yourself going into your resource state at the sight of your boss. Or the stimulus may generalize to trigger a resource state whenever anyone raises his/her voice at you. You may find yourself spending more and more time in a resource state as the stimuli for the state increase through the process of generalization.

The more you stay in your resource state, the easier it will be for you to gain your outcomes. When you are acting spontaneously, with great confidence—as most of us do in our resource states—you have a lifetime of stored resources at your command. You are more flexible in responding because you are aware of other possible courses of action.

Using a resource state has changed many people's lives in dramatic ways—mine, for one. Do not underestimate how powerful it can be. If you are not able to get a strong emotional surge when you say your word and imagine your circle, find a friend, and try the process again at a later time. You are entitled to a state of excellence that runs quickly, smoothly, and effortlessly. Indulge yourself.

In the next chapter you will learn how to intensify and expand your resource state and how to stack resource states to counteract a strong negative stimulus.

Generalization occurs when a new pattern of response spreads out its association to similar events, people, stimuli.

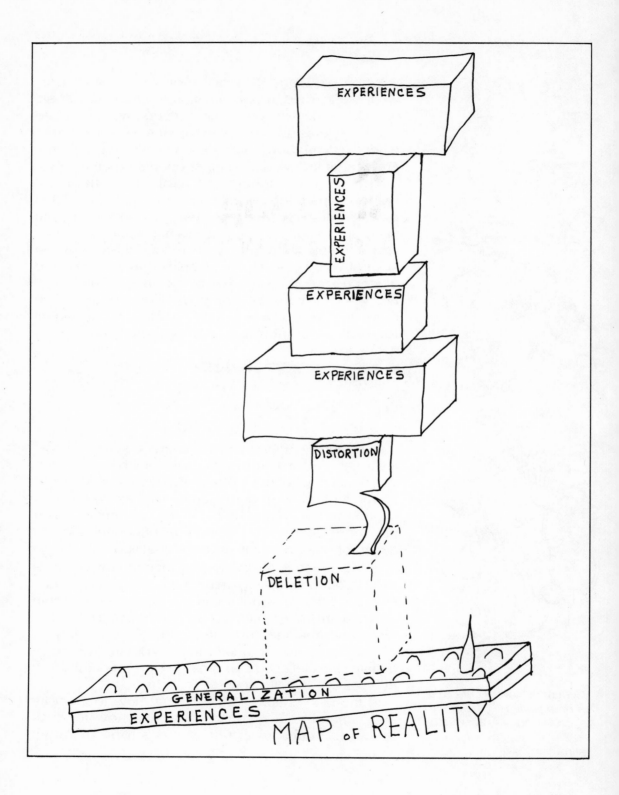

10
Stacking
Resource States

Now you have learned how to create a resource state, but you may be wondering if that state will provide the counterbalance you need to deal with a powerful, negative response—one that has been well established through painful experience. Or, suppose you had difficulty setting up a resource state as you followed the steps in Chapter 9.

If you find that your resource state is not working as well as you would like in a specific situation, or if you had trouble selecting an extraordinary accomplishment in the previous chapter, you can stack memories of several positive events to create or intensify your resource state—to fire off the electrical and chemical reactions in your brain associated with a state of excellence. No one knows why, but if you add enough positive memories together, they can offset even weighty negatives. It may be Freud's pleasure principle at work. You do not need to know *why* in order to enjoy the results.

Freud's pleasure principle, simply stated: We prefer and will select pleasure over pain when both options are perceived as possible.

STACK YOUR RESOURCES

To stack resource states, first think of a time you did something very well. If you have no clear memory of accomplishing something extraordinary, use the best memory you have. Then go through the step-by-step sequence outlined in Chapter 9.

You do not have to understand why a telephone works in order to dial a number.

Next, think of another time you felt really pleased with something you had accomplished. (The two events do not have to be related.) Select a code word for this second event. When you are able to see, hear, and feel the second event, take a deep breath, say your *two* code words (one for each memory), and step into the circle. Do not just imagine the step; actually take it physically as you move into the circle mentally. Imagine the circle if you wish, but physically move—step inside the circle.

If you are not feeling great yet, step out of the circle, and recall a *third* time you did something so well you surprised yourself. Go through the see, hear, feel process on that memory as well, and select a code word for the third memory. Then say the *three* code words (one for each memory), take a deep breath, and step inside the circle. You may use the same circle each time, but select three distinctive code words so you will have all three to use as stimuli.

If for any reason the process of stacking resource states does not work for you—if you do not feel a change—read the rest of this book and try again. If the process still does not work, write to me. I will get you an appointment with someone who is trained to help people who are having difficulty creating a resource state.

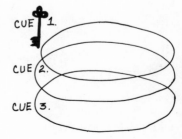

An Antidote to Jealousy

Jealousy affects business as well as personal relationships. Those of you who suffer from jealousy never seem to notice that it does not show its green head when you are feeling secure. I have worked with a number of suffering clients, and I have noticed that the two internal states cancel each other out: If you are secure, you are not jealous; if you are jealous, you are not secure.

A simple thought process can bring instant security. You already know the process—it is a form of stacking your resources. Here is the way to use jealousy to increase your security.

Each time you notice you are feeling even a twinge of jealousy, remember a time when someone gave you a compliment about yourself that you know to be true. For example, someone may have said, with sincerity, "What beautiful eyes you have." Remember that person's voice, facial expression, and your feelings when you heard that remark.

Select two more positive memories about your self-worth. Give those memories colors, sounds, and feelings for a few moments, allowing them to work their magic. Then store the memories where you can retrieve them easily.

Check your feelings now. The jealousy should be diminished or totally gone. The next time you feel a twinge of jealousy, you can use the same memories or choose three new, positive ones. Stack these self-worth memories on top of one another so you can say to yourself a word like "terrific," and all your pictures, sounds, and feelings will be available, in quick sequence, to your conscious mind. The mental gymnastic is: Jealousy → 1. Self-worth
2. Self-worth
3. Self-worth

Soon you can turn the stimulus of jealousy into the stimulus of self-worth.

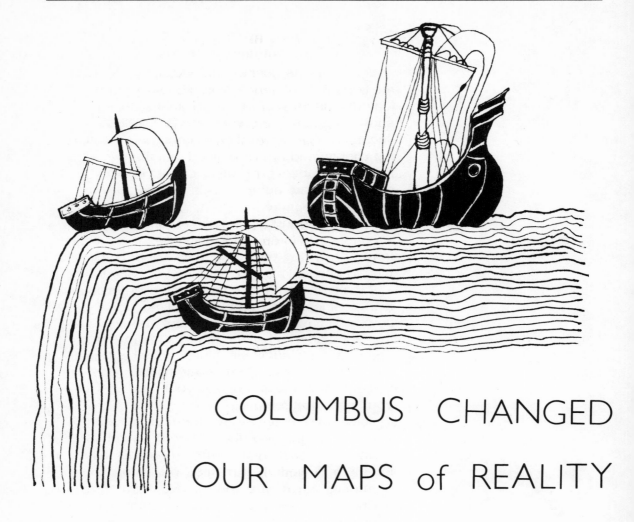

COLUMBUS CHANGED
OUR MAPS of REALITY

All of us have different belief systems—different maps of reality. Each of these maps has been created by memories coded with the help of deletion,
                                    distortion,
                                        generalization.

Our different maps mean we need more than one way to set up a resource state. You may need to experiment with the basic ingredients to create your own resource state.

EXCELLENCE CAN BE HABIT FORMING

How do you remember to call up your resource state—your state of excellence—when you are in a difficult situation? When you are under fire, how do you find time to say your word and imagine your circle?

Practice. The more often you trigger your state of excellence, the more likely it is to fire when you need it. Remember J. C. Eccles's observation: There is "an enduring enhancement of synaptic efficacy with usage." In other words, habits are more likely to occur than new behaviors. Habitual thinking patterns are more likely to fire than new synaptic pathways—new thinking patterns. Turn your state of excellence into a habit by using it often.

Not a good idea—to try to change people who do not want to change

A Word for Skeptics

Those of you with a strong skeptical part (like me) may not believe this can work. If you did not go through the steps outlined in Chapter 9, you may be saying, "I don't believe this will work, and if I don't believe it, it won't work."

What we believe does affect our perceptions, our thinking, our behavior. But even if you think the process cannot work, I encourage you to try it. Follow the sequence given on page 170. You will probably find that a resource state—a state of excellence—occurs. The physiological shift seems to be strong enough to overcome a lack of belief.

In business seminars, when I teach how to set up a resource state, I first explain the process and the desired outcome. Then I ask for a volunteer who does *not* believe the process will work. (There is *always* a volunteer.) And 99 times in 100, even though people are watching and the subject has declared his/her belief that the process does not work, it still works. Why this particular process is stronger than our belief systems I do not know. Perhaps the process actually changes closely held beliefs about our capability to switch internal states easily and quickly. Fortunately, we can benefit from resource states without understanding exactly how they work.

In eight years of teaching people how to create resource states, I have had difficulty only a few times. One volunteer, an engineer, refused to try the process because, as he put it, "I'm comfortable with the way my head works, and I do not want to mess it up." This individual's boss had already been through my seminar and had enrolled his subordinate because he wanted him to learn these skills. So I decided to try something else. I asked the engineer if he would try the process later at home alone. He said he thought he might, after he had considered all the implications. I left it at that.

Use your resource state for

interviews
negotiations
presentations
performance reviews
sales
irate customers
meetings
conflicts
coaching
asking for a raise

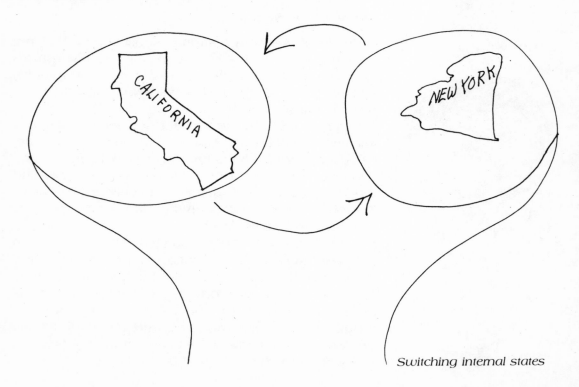

Switching internal states

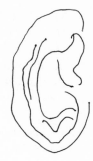

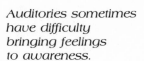

*Auditories sometimes
have difficulty
bringing feelings
to awareness.*

In another seminar, I had a volunteer whose primary sense was auditory: He gathered most of his information about the world from what he heard. This man's kinesthetic awareness was so slight that the change to a resource state did not seem dramatic. When he stepped into his circle, he said he could feel a slight change, but nothing really significant.

I had taught this process successfully so many times that I was surprised. I was concerned that the entire class would follow his example. I took a deep breath, then asked two other volunteers to demonstrate their resource states so the audience could see the dramatic changes that can occur. They were both successful, and now the class had role models. Each person in the seminar was then able to create a state of excellence.

Another time one volunteer said, "This is not working for me," as he stepped out of the circle. Yet, while in the circle he had straightened his posture, lifted his chin, changed color, and altered his breathing rate. I looked at the audience, who had noted the changes. They all seemed mystified. When I said nothing—simply looked puzzled, too—he repeated, "This just doesn't work for me."

"Oh," I said. "Let's you and I try some other approaches while the others are setting up their resource states." He already had his resource state, but he wasn't aware of it. In 10 minutes I taught him how to be aware.

How can one not be aware of a drastic emotional change? Auditories sometimes have difficulty bringing feeling to awareness; yet this participant was not an auditory. He was a kinesthetic who had denied his body responses for so many years that he barely felt them. This kind of unawareness is not that rare in the business world. If you suspect that you are unaware, spend a day writing down your internal states (emotions) every 5 minutes (for example, curious, bored, sleepy, anxious, scared, content, peaceful, joyful, happy). At the end of the day, you will know a lot more about yourself.

Your feelings are high-quality information—a scorecard of how you are doing in life.

IF YOU DRAW A BLANK

A few people may have no conscious memories of feeling extraordinarily successful or competent. But some of them can recall someone they know who performed extraordinarily well or attained high achievements. These people can access a resource state by imagining themselves performing in the same way, with the same feelings. Others who have difficulty remembering feelings of special accomplishment may be able to identify with sports heroes, historical figures, or film characters who have achieved special goals. By using another's experience, these individuals can go through the step-by-step process and create a resource state. Once they have done this and begin operating from a resource state, they will have their own successful experiences to draw on to reinforce that state.

Room going sour

Recognizing you are in trouble the moment it occurs gives you time to do something else.

On occasion, even in your resource state, you may find a situation is not working out the way you expect. I had a problem once when teaching an important business seminar. I suddenly realized that the room had gone sour. I had taught the material before at this company and had had good results. Now, somehow, I had turned off several participants, and these people were negatively affecting the others. I knew I was in trouble.

In such a situation I am programmed to go immediately into my resource state, in which I stand with my weight evenly distributed. My normal teaching posture is weight on the left foot, head tilted slightly. So I shifted my weight, and when I felt my resource state click into place, I tried a joke. It failed miserably. I then switched to an old gestalt truism: "State the obvious and probe for outcomes." I said, "I see some of you look unhappy. What would you like?"

Several people looked puzzled; they were not unhappy. Some people looked relieved; they sensed that something was amiss. Two or three individuals looked ready to fight. They were the source of the problem in the room. One of these said, "I would like something substantial." "How would you know if it were substantial?" I asked. "It would be something I could use today," she answered.

Because I had been teaching skills that could be used that very day, I was speechless. If she did not know that the skills were to be put into use immediately, I was *not* doing a good job of teaching. But my resource state was in place. I checked it carefully, and I was still speechless. At that moment my partner arrived, as scheduled, to take over the class. His arrival broke the spell, and the rest of the day went splendidly. I was able to teach a later section of the same group and regain rapport. It is comforting to know that you can survive even if your resource state fails. This was the only time in eight years of seminar training that my resource state did not get me out of difficulty.

You may be curious to know what I would have done if my partner had not arrived. I could have asked the participant with the "substantial" demand to volunteer for a problem-solving demonstration directly related to a current situation she was in. Or I could have selected the leader in the room and demonstrated how to create a resource state—out of sequence in the seminar workbook, but possibly a good move. Finally, I might have suggested a coffee break, because we usually change mental position when we change body position. Clearly, what I had been doing was *not* working, so I needed to do something else.

Although the resource state is a very useful tool, it will not solve every difficulty you encounter in your life. It will provide you with resources to help you respond to challenging situations in new and more creative ways. I know that in my resource state, as compared to my normal alert state, I am

- More effective in gaining my outcome
- More sensitive to people and events around me
- More confident in my responses
- More appropriate in my words and behaviors
- More creative in finding unexpected solutions to sudden glitches in interactions

A person in a state of excellence is like a tree, deeply rooted, leaves and branches responding to changing conditions.

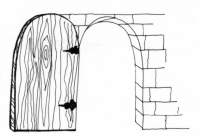

Door to the unconscious?

NEW DIRECTIONS

I am going to go out on a limb here and express a theory about resource states, based on my own experiences. I do not know how to prove or disprove the validity of this theory. Here it is: *The state of excellence is the door to our unconscious.* I believe that past learnings not organized in a way to be retrieved consciously can be retrieved quickly and effortlessly in a state of excellence.

Why? I do have one or two clues, but I have not solved the mystery. However, here is an example of how I used unconscious resources while in a state of excellence to "turn around" a situation in which all the cards were stacked against success. This experience occurred when I sorted out a problem at one of the Fortune 100 companies—I'll call it JCO.

A senior educator at JCO had read *Influencing with Integrity* and had incorporated several of the skills from the book into a five-day seminar he had created for the company's engineers. Reactions were favorable, and the seminar was very successful, until another JCO employee began trying to convert his colleagues to neurolinguistic techniques in offensive ways. This proselytizer turned

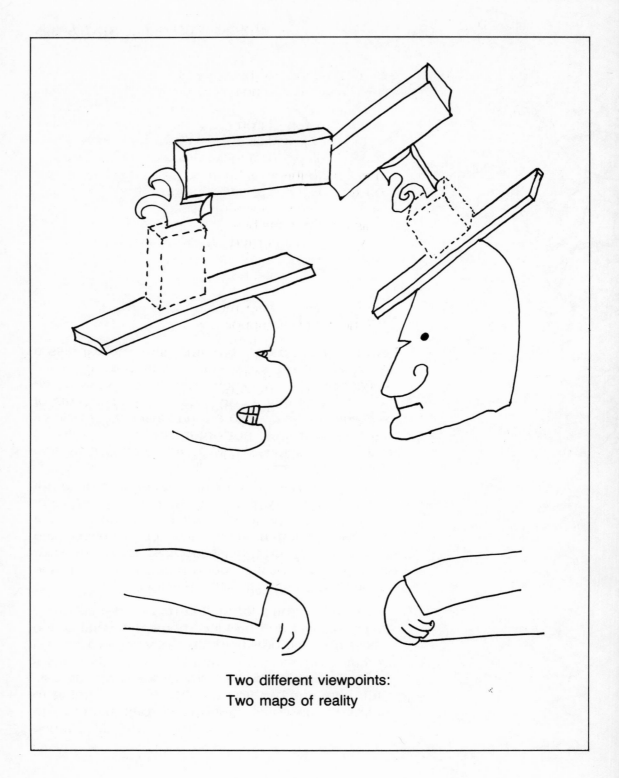

Two different viewpoints:
Two maps of reality

Map of reality

off so many people by his behavior that the official word came down—no more of that flaky stuff in JCO seminars.

My champion put on his white hat and set out to defend neurolinguistics, his seminar, and me—in that order. He suggested to his boss's boss that before an edict like this was handed down, more information on the subject of neurolinguistics would be useful. He sent copies of *Influencing with Integrity* to his boss and his boss's boss; then he called me. He was so concerned about the situation that I offered to help in any way I could. (I had in mind telephone meetings, but he heard my offer another way.)

He decided to offer me up to his boss's boss; in fact, he set up an appointment. The fact that I had to travel through four time zones to keep the appointment did not deter him from his offering; his seminar was in jeopardy. When my champion called to tell me about the appointment, I demurred. He reminded me that I had promised to do whatever I could to help him present the case for neurolinguistics.

I bought an airline ticket, flew across the country, rented a car, and arrived in upstate New York at 9 a.m.—at the lion's den, the place the earth fell away, the sea of despond. (The metaphors ran rampant through my brain that cold winter morning. The landscape outside the office building was beige, the sky was grey, the trees were bare.) The most appropriate metaphor for that meeting was a tanker dodging a destroyer, submerged icebergs, and lethal underwater mines. I was the tanker, the boss's boss was the destroyer, and the innocent-looking modern office was a sea of icebergs and underwater mines.

Mr. X began, his expression serious, "I spent some time last week calling people in JCO who attended your public seminars."

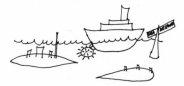

I thought, "Uh-oh, which people did he reach?" I had taught a lot of people in my seminars, some from JCO. Which ones was he reporting on? I could feel the icebergs. I could sense the underwater mines. I decided to say nothing. I tried a small smile of encouragement, but it died from lack of nourishment. I waited. The pause lengthened.

He barked, "Some of them have never used what you taught in the seminar."

I looked steadily back at him, shrugged slightly to let him know that I had heard him, and my expression said, "That's sad." My mouth said nothing.

He relented a bit, "Some of them liked your information." Pause. "Some of them even said they used it." Pause. "Some of them said they have forgotten all about it and did not know whether it worked or not." Long pause.

"Yes, well, that's education. You win some. You lose some." Not brilliant, Genie.

He nodded, but he did not smile. I did not smile, or nod. He asked abruptly, "How does your organization of this material keep it from being manipulative? That is, I understand, your claim."

Now I nodded. "Yes, I claim that. I claim that if you are willing to find out the other's outcome and attempt to satisfy it—at the same time that you are attempting to gain your own outcome, in a way that you both benefit—then you are influencing, not manipulating."

He barked, "Are you doing that now?"

"Doing what now?"

"Finding out my outcome?"

"Not yet."

"When will you?"

"When we have enough rapport to begin."

"What is your definition of rapport?" Gruff. Gruff. Billy Goat Gruff. New metaphor.

"Trust in competence for the task at hand."

"What is the task at hand?"

Recognizing process, as well as content, is the key to successful communication.

Some processes of
communication:

rapport

nonrapport

trust

nontrust

moving toward

  outcomes

stuck

dovetailing

bulldozing

energizing

frustrating

gathering data

stonewalling

sending data

stonewalling

small talk

nitty gritty

"To establish my competence."

Long silence. Begrudgingly, "I think you are competent."

I replied, "I think you are competent."

Long pause. He barked, "What now?"

"The task changes," I growled.

"To what?"

"Will JCO people benefit from the neurolinguistic skills in the seminar?" My voice was a low growl.

"What do *you* have to say to that?" His voice relented a little.

"Have you read the evaluations from the people who have completed the seminar?"

"Yes."

"I rest my case."

"What is your outcome?" He had done his homework. He was using my language to establish rapport with me. This was an unexpected shift. The underwater mines were defused, the icebergs thawing—still floating around, but smaller.

"I'd like to sell my materials to JCO."

"We don't have any money in this year's budget."

"Fine. I'll wait until next year." This was February. It would be a long wait. Then I realized that JCO's use of my materials for ten months would jeopardize my copyright. So I asked, "How about a $1 fee for the use of the material during the remainder of the scheduled seminars?"

I got a $1 check. Then in May I sold JCO a program for $20,000.

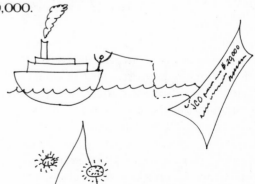

During this entire interaction, I was in my resource state, responding quickly and almost without conscious internal computations. There was no time to consider lots of answers and select one. The questions were barked quickly, and long waits for answers would not have worked. I was retrieving skills from my unconscious faster than my conscious mind could compute. My state of excellence turned a planned "sinking" into a success. I believe I won that day because I was able to quickly retrieve unconscious behaviors that were appropriate responses to a difficult situation.

You think quickly in a resource state.

I think of a state of excellence this way: When I remember a time I did something extraordinarily well, I activate the pattern laid down originally in my brain by that extraordinary performance. The chemicals—the spatial-temporal pattern in my neurology—are activated by that act of memory. Once activated, this resource state pattern allows me to access other information—patterns not available in my conscious state. The state of excellence pattern activates other patterns that are appropriate at that moment. Why do the chemicals and patterns of the state of excellence do this? I do not know. I do know that by going into a resource state I become much more effective in choosing behaviors that will gain my outcome.

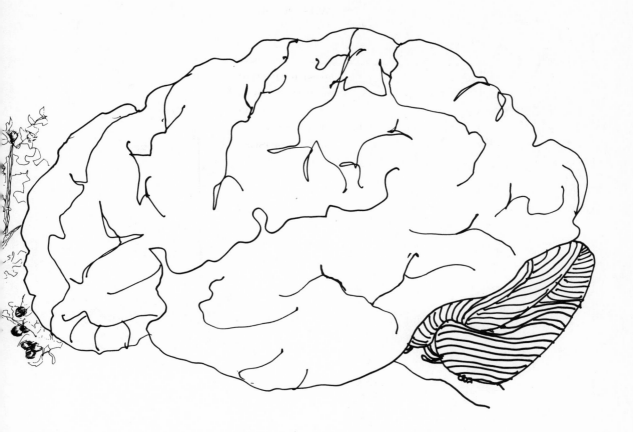

Using the stimulus-response mechanism to intensify your resource state gives you a very powerful tool. Another powerful tool is introduced in the next chapter. You will learn how to switch response patterns, to give your brain a choice when you hook a new positive response pattern to an old stimulus that produced a negative response. I call this process "switching marquees."

*In surveys, most people rank fear of making a presentation
higher than fear of death.*

11
Switching Marquees

What do you do if your response to a stimulus is not the response you want? Suppose you are making a telephone sales call, and your prospect is rude and hangs up abruptly. How would you respond? Would you become upset and not make any more calls that day? Would you postpone your next call and read the newspaper—perhaps the want ads? Would you shrug your shoulders and go on to the next customer? Whatever your response, is it the one you want in this situation?

Remember Eccles's concept of the brain as a theater marquee? Once you know how to create a resource state, you can use the same process to switch your response pattern. You can choose which lights go on and which do not. Because you can light up any response you want to a given stimulus, you can switch from an old, negative response to a new, positive one. So if your response is not the one you want in a particular situation, you can change it.

Same cat, new response

CHANGING A RESPONSE

One of my clients, Brenda, came to me for help with a response she did not want. Whenever she had to make an important presentation to senior management, she froze. Brenda was a poised, attractive, well-dressed woman in her mid-thirties. She appeared both competent and confident. She had just been promoted to a senior management position— the only woman in her company to reach that level.

After Brenda and I had chatted for a while and established rapport, I asked, "What would you like?"

"I have to make a presentation to senior level management on Monday, and I'm scared."

"What, specifically, does 'scared' feel like to you?" I asked.

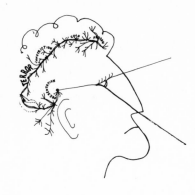

"My throat gets tight. I can't find words. I don't seem to be able to breathe. I'm frozen. I feel cold all over."

I reached over and lightly touched the back of Brenda's left hand as she went through this description. She was focusing so intently on her feelings that she did not seem to notice the touch. If she did notice, she may have thought it was an empathic gesture. I made a sweeping motion with my hand as if erasing a chalkboard. "OK. Let that feeling go, and tell me about a time you did something really well."

"What sort of thing?" Brenda sounded slightly indignant. She found my question difficult to respond to because she was still feeling the physical effects of the internal search that had elicited such strong negatives.

"Any time in your memory when you did something really well. Do you play tennis? Golf? What do you do really well?"

A short silence, then, "I'm a really good cook."

"Good. Do you remember a time when you prepared a delicious dish, you knew it, and someone told you how good it was?"

"Not someone—a whole bunch of people."

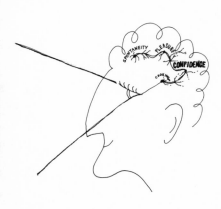

"Can you picture the expressions on their faces?" I asked.

She nodded.

"Can you hear what they are saying?"

She nodded.

"Can you remember your feelings?"

As she nodded, Brenda's face filled with color, and I placed two of my fingertips softly on the back of her right hand. She noticed this touch. I said, "I'm using the stimulus-response mechanism. I'm going to set up a new sequence for you that will be more useful than your old sequence of feeling scared when you make a presentation."

"How are you going to do this?" There was no opposition in her voice, only curiosity.

"I'm setting up new cues for some old patterns that are already laid down in your neurology. Then I'm going to link a cue to a response you already have so you can make your presentation and enjoy the entire thing."

Her expression said, "I don't believe you."

I matched her facial expression with these words: "I know you don't believe this is possible. You are about to learn how to do something new. That's why you're here, isn't it? I'm not going to do anything but teach you a new skill. You are going to do the work."

Brenda looked relieved. She was willing to learn from me, but not willing to have me do something to her. I agreed with her. I do not like people doing things to me. I do like to learn new things. I continued, "OK. I've set up, I think, cues for two different responses already laid down in your brain and in your neurology."

"When?"

"Oh, while you were talking. Now let's check to see if the cues are working." I reached over and touched the back of her left hand. Her expression became similar to the negative, frozen one she had had earlier.

"Yes, that's in there. Did you notice the frozen response, the scared one, the one you want to get rid of when you make the presentation?" I asked this question only so Brenda would know that the cue had been set up. I had already noted her expression and knew the cue was hooked to a specific response.

"Yes," she answered with enough anxiety in her voice to confirm that the response was strong.

I made the same sweeping gesture with my hand that I had made earlier—the erasing motion. I was interrupting Brenda's pattern so she would not stay in the negative state any longer than was necessary.

Pace, then lead.

You can write whatever coming attractions you want on your marquee.

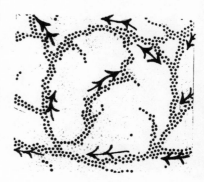

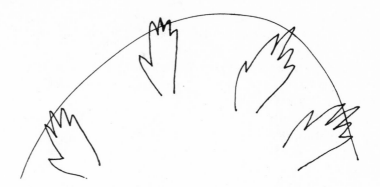

"Now let's see if the other cue is set up." I reached over and placed two fingertips on the back of her right hand. Immediately, her color changed and her face softened.

"Are you remembering the delicious dish and the feeling of doing something really well?" I asked.

"Yes." As Brenda said this, her expression indicated that the memory had intensified in some way, and the response now appeared strong enough to counteract the negative response.

Earlier, I had planned to stack Brenda's responses of excellence because I was not sure that the memory of the cooking experience would be strong enough to counter the extreme negative feelings she had about making a presentation. However, seeing her strong response, I decided to try this one cue-key. Her strong response gave me confidence that the pattern was well set up. The natural brain processes seemed to be doing their work.

"Good. Now we are going to switch responses. We are going to give you a choice. You can feel either scared or competent, the way you felt when you cooked that meal. I'm betting that your neurons will choose to fire off the cooking pattern. Your brain cells will decide whether you feel good or bad when you make your presentation."

Anchors Aweigh

Some people know stimulus-response patterning as anchoring, and stimuli are sometimes called anchors. Anchors feel heavy, and anchoring feels even heavier to me. Because changing old patterns seems to be a lightening up—not a heavying (weighing) down—I prefer these new terms:

anchors: *cue-keys*

anchoring: *marqueeing*

collapsing anchors:
  switching marquees

Of course, she did not believe me. I did not expect her to. If I had been in her shoes, I would not have believed it either.

"OK," I said. "Would you close your eyes? I'm going to touch both cues at once. You pay attention to what happens."

I touched the back of each hand simultaneously, and the negative and positive expressions played vividly back and forth across her face, one after the other, like a marquee lighting up first with one name and then another—first one pattern, then the other, then the first again. After 20 seconds, the positive expression won, and her eyes popped opened with a startled look.

She said, "You wouldn't believe what that was like."

I looked at her questioningly.

"Well, maybe *you* would. *I* can't believe what it was like."

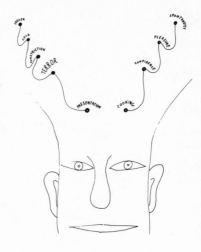

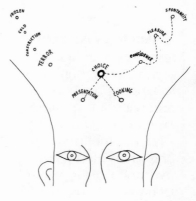

STIMULUS-RESPONSES
presentation—confidence
pleasure
spontaneity

I knew Brenda needed some time to regain her balance after this intense experience, so I said:

"Let me tell you about the Navy captain who linked a cat to an orderly. The captain was in a seminar in which I had just taught this particular skill, which I call 'switching marquees.' He wanted to change his feelings of irritation toward a certain enlisted man who reported to him twice a week. The man's report, which should have taken 5 minutes, always took 30 minutes. The captain had tried every ploy he knew to shorten the presentation, but nothing worked. Because the captain could not change the enlisted man, he decided to change his own internal response.

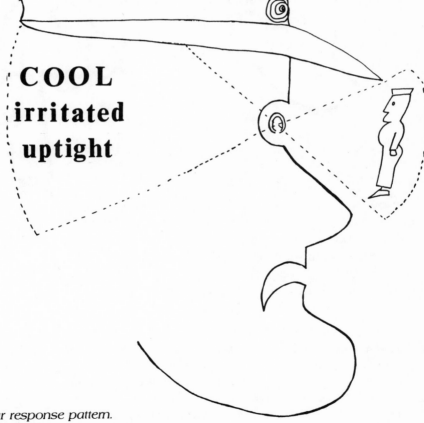

COOL
irritated
uptight

You can change your response pattern.

"The captain had a cat he liked. The cat would meet him at his door every night after work. The captain would sit down, stroke the cat, and relax. The captain decided to hook the cat-relax response to the sailor-irritated response. It worked almost too well. So well, in fact, that his seminar partner called me over because the captain became upset.

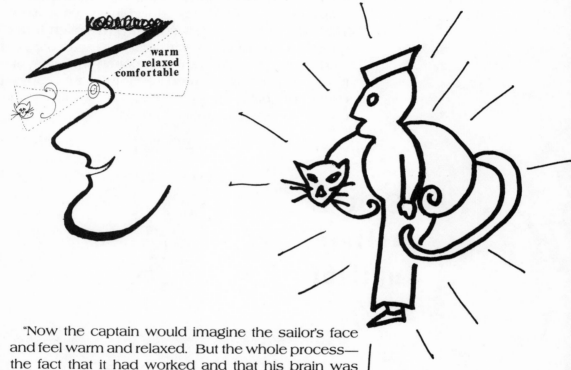

warm
relaxed
comfortable

"Now the captain would imagine the sailor's face and feel warm and relaxed. But the whole process— the fact that it had worked and that his brain was so flexible—affected the captain adversely. I persuaded him that his brain was working fine, but I cautioned him about getting carried away and stroking the sailor."

My story had given Brenda time to recover. Now she knew that other people were susceptible to this experience—even tough Navy captains.

"But what will happen when I make the presentation on Monday?" she asked.

"I don't know for sure. You now have a choice of two responses. Whenever we have a choice, our

Be careful of what you decide to change: these techniques work.

brains seem to choose a positive rather than a negative response. Let's check and see which choice you make. Can you imagine yourself giving the presentation?"

Brenda was making internal pictures. "Yes."

I asked, "What's happening?"

"I feel OK. But I'm not really doing it now. I'm only imagining it."

"You're right."

"So I won't really know whether this has worked or not until I make the presentation?" she asked.

"*You* may not know it until then," I said. "But I can tell you now, it works. I can see your face as you're imagining the presentation, and the scared look is no longer there. Let's go into the hall so you can look in the mirror as you think about Monday. That may convince you."

Brenda imagined the presentation while looking in the mirror, but she was still not convinced, so we agreed that she would call me Monday night. When she called, she said that, although she had not enjoyed the presentation, she had performed well. She had been able to breathe, to talk, to think on her feet. She had not felt her usual fright.

I suggested that Brenda add another positive stimulus-response to the good-cooking pattern, one related to a memory of total enjoyment. Similar to stacking resource states, described in Chapter 10, adding another positive stimulus-response experience would strengthen and reinforce the good feelings.

GIVING YOUR BRAIN A CHOICE

By using the stimulus-response mechanism—the same mechanism Pavlov used—Brenda was able to change her response pattern. She had had two responses— one positive, one negative—to two different stimuli. After she hooked the two stimulus-responses together, her brain had to choose between one response and the other. A fortunate thing about the brain is that, given a choice, it will choose the option that feels better.

This choice may be related to what Sigmund Freud called the "pleasure principle": The brain chooses pleasure over pain whenever either response is possible. Once there are connecting patterns, the pattern that wins is the one that produces pleasure or positive feelings, rather than the one that produces pain or negative feelings. The negative response is still laid down in the neurons of the brain. It has not disappeared. But the positive pattern will win out as long as a positive response is hooked to the same stimulus.

MARQUEES

When you realize this about the brain, you will be able to use this skill to eliminate unwanted emotional states; you will be able to switch marquees. All you have to do is hook up each unwanted emotional state to a wanted emotional state, and the positive state will win out. You will still retain the resources you have learned from those "negative" experiences, as well as from those experiences for which you have not found an appropriate use. Negative experiences are valuable for whatever learning took place. With a new choice of responses, however, the negative, or unwanted, response need no longer fire whenever the stimulus occurs. Now you have a choice.

There are few truly negative response patterns. Most learning is potentially useful. There are, however, inappropriate responses. Change to appropriate responses and the entire pattern becomes positive.

Switching marquees is use-
ful for many negative mental states.

HOW TO SWITCH MARQUEES

Here is the way to hook a positive stimulus-response pattern to a negative one—to switch marquees—so that the positive response becomes the preferred choice:

1. Close your eyes, and think of a time when a certain stimulus triggered a response you no longer want without a choice.
2. When you can see, hear, and feel the entire unwanted experience, touch yourself somewhere with one finger. (You are setting up kinesthetic cue-key 1.)
3. Think of another response you would like to have to the stimulus in step 1.
4. When you can see, hear, and feel the entire wanted experience, touch yourself somewhere with one finger, this time on the opposite side of your body so you can keep the two cue-keys separate. (You are setting up kinesthetic cue-key 2.)
5. Touch cue-key 1, and see if you recall the unwanted experience. As soon as you feel the response, open your eyes and come back to the present. In other words, break off the unwanted memory.
6. Next, touch cue-key 2, and see if you recall the wanted experience. Again, interrupt the memory when you are satisfied that the cue-key is set.

   If either cue-key is not set, start over, intensifying the sensory data—what you saw, heard, and felt in the original experience. Do not dissociate. Keep yourself in the response. By making your pictures clearer, the colors brighter, you can intensify your feelings. If you make the voices and sounds louder, you may intensify your feelings even more. Play around with the smells and tastes of the memory as well, until you

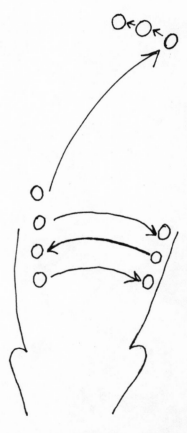

Some people say it feels like a Ping-Pong ball in your brain.

obtain the intense feeling you want. Then check each cue-key again to be sure you are getting two responses.

7. Now touch both cue-keys at once. You may wish to close your eyes as you do this.

Different people report different responses during step 7. Many see pictures of the two experiences flash back and forth in sequence until the positive feelings win out. For some people nothing dramatic happens. In such cases a change has sometimes occurred, but sometimes not. However, you can rest assured that the unwanted response has not attached itself to cue-key 2, the positive stimulus.

AUDITORIES are special.
We have one at our house.

Sometimes this kinesthetic switching technique does not work with pure auditories. One way I tailor this process for them is to use sounds instead of touches as cue-keys. I have used a small gong to mark the unwanted response and another gong for the wanted response. Striking both gongs, in sequence, makes the process work. Any two sounds can be used as cue-keys (e.g., a whistle and a clap). Nonverbal sounds seem to be more effective than words or touches for auditories.

8. To check whether or not you have switched marquees, imagine a future time when the stimulus in step 1 would be present. Notice if your new response fires off automatically. It should. If your new response does not fire off, stack a new positive on top of the old positive; then begin again with step 1.

Auditories may need special cues—

gongs
whistles
claps
music

Remember that the positive, wanted response has to be stronger, bigger, better, and clearer than the negative, or unwanted, response, or the switch will not occur. You may need to stack one or more positive responses to get the result you want.

To offset a powerful negative response pattern, you can stack positive, wanted experiences on top of one another until the total of all the positive experiences outweighs the unwanted pattern. Set up cue-keys for each separate, wanted experience, and then hook them all together by touching them at the same time with the tip of each of your fingers. Then you will have a strong response pattern with lots of positive feelings.

The ability to set up a resource state any time you need it and the ability to change any unwanted pattern to a wanted pattern are very powerful skills.

Negative responses to—

cluttered desks
husbands' voices
bosses
mothers-in-law
vegetables
traffic jams
Monday morning
suitcases—

have succumbed to the switching marquees technique.

CHANGE HISTORY

Change history is a variation of marqueeing that is fun and has long-lasting results. *Change history* is a way to edit your memories—your history movies—and give them the happy ending that was missing in the original release.

Here is a mnemonic to help you remember the steps in editing your own memory films:

C Collect related painful memories

H Have a friend set up cue-keys

A Arrange cue-keys in sequence

N Notice the *see* data, *hear* data, *feel* data

G Generate a search for new endings

E Entertain yourself

H Have a friend cue-key positive endings

I Install positive cue-keys with *see, hear, feel* data

S Sequences should match (for example, left forearm and right forearm)

T Test by touching negative and positive cue-keys

O One set at a time (left arm, right arm) until all memories are edited

R Responses are your history and your present

Y Your memories are more useful when edited for pleasure viewing

This man needs a change.

Let's look at these memory-editing steps in detail.

Collect related painful memories. All of us have painful experiences that we have coded in our brains in pictures, sounds, smells, tastes, and feelings. What we forget when we remember these past events is that we have added the pain to what went on in the pictures, sounds, smells, and tastes.

Here is an example. When Joe first began selling, he had a number of rejections, no-sales, even some brusque dismissals. He also had a few successes. The "no-sales" seemed to carry more emotional impact, however, than the successes. After a while, Joe found himself reluctant to pick up the phone to make an appointment for a sales call. He found himself doing busywork rather than making sales calls.

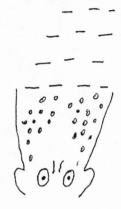

Clearly, Joe's history was coloring his present behavior. Time for *change history*. He showed up at 9 a.m. on the dot. He was ready.

Have a friend set up cue-keys. Arrange cue-keys in sequence. Notice *see, hear, feel* data. I told Joe to remember three separate painful experiences connected with sales. As he recounted later, he saw in his mind's eye the first office, the first rejecting person, his briefcase; then he heard the voices; then he felt the failure. As he recalled these sensory components, I touched a spot on his left forearm and said, "In a moment, we'll check to be sure the cue-key is set."

I waited a moment, then touched the spot again, watching for his response. He said, "Yes, that's the experience. I still feel bad about it. I hate failure."

I replied, "Now find another painful experience."

As Joe remembered two other rejections, I established two additional cue-keys—one midway down his forearm, another on his wrist.

Generate a search for new endings. Entertain yourself. Joe began to think of sales calls that had had happy endings. He played some memories of successful ventures unrelated to sales: Teachers who praised his papers; lovers who told him he was special; his father, who thought he was a great son. He enjoyed his memory trip and felt much better after the positive movies. Then he selected three memories that had some relationship to the negative cue-keys established.

Have a friend cue-key positive endings. Install positive cue-keys with *see, hear, feel* data. Sequences should match. The first failure Joe experienced resulted from being new in the sales business and not having a list of clients. He needed a track record for credibility. The positive cue-key he used to change this painful memory was another, more recent scene in which another sales representative had said, his voice full of admiration, "What really impresses me is that you sold Chase Manhattan Bank."

Joe remembered the sales rep's face, voice, and words and his own glow of accomplishment, for, indeed, he had made an impressive sale. I set up this positive cue-key high on Joe's right forearm, opposite its negative partner on the left forearm.

Joe's next painful experience was one in which the client had been totally uninterested in his presentation and just sat there, barely containing his boredom, until Joe finished. His positive match for that was a more recent memory of a 30-minute presentation that lasted 3 hours, followed by lunch. They later signed a contract. As Joe remembered this positive experience, I set up a cue-key midway down his forearm.

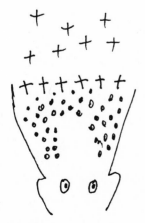

It's your choice.

The last painful experience was one in which Joe had underpriced a product so that he actually lost money on the chance of future business, which never materialized. He was not only rejected, but royally taken advantage of. The positive experience to counteract this negative experience was a picture of his financial statement, his accountant saying, "You had a good year," and the feeling of satisfaction he had because his business was becoming more successful each year. I set up this cue-key on Joe's wrist.

Test by touching negative and positive cue-keys. One set at a time. I tested each cue-key to be sure each was set up. Then I touched the first negative and its matching positive at the same time. Joe smiled. Next I touched the second negative with its matching positive. Joe hummed. Then I checked the third negative and the third positive cue-key. Joe sort of laughed—a small laugh, but a definite laugh.

Joe said he was resisting the urge to go to the telephone and make an appointment with someone for a sales presentation. We were not quite finished, but Joe was ready to move. I decided we were finished, he thanked me, and went straight to his office to make his calls.

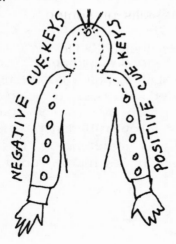

Responses are your history and your present. Your memories are more useful when edited for pleasure viewing. Our present behaviors are greatly dependent on how we feel about ourselves. Our feelings of self-worth, confidence, and competence are based on our memories. Our memories are constructs of what actually happened; deletion, distortion, and generalization are rampant in them. We might as well operate in the present from memories that are beneficial.

"Stop!" you might say. "Aren't you living a lie if you pretend the past was wonderful when it was terrible?" Actually, when you use the *change history* technique you do not change the essential components—the see, hear, smell, and taste data. You change the way you feel about those sensory components. In some cases, your past feelings are no longer helpful—if they ever were. You can make them useful by adding new pieces to the history record.

This ability to add what you know now to what you knew then is a natural ability and one I cherish. It gives us a more balanced appraisal of our own worth. We may not be perfect, but we can learn. *Change history* is a way to use learning on past experiences as well as on present ones.

The change skills presented thus far have proceeded from simple to advanced. The next chapter presents the most advanced technique of all, which is to be used on intense fears and phobias. If Brenda's scared feeling had been extreme, close to terror, I would have chosen this technique for her.

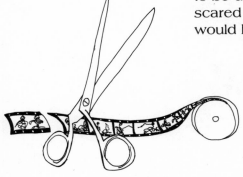

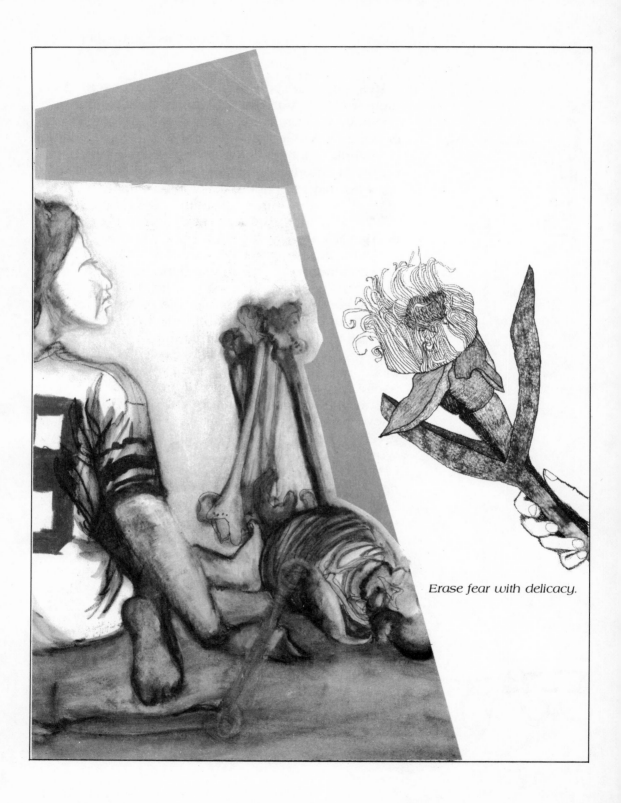

Erase fear with delicacy.

12
Unlearning Fear

Snakes, spiders, heights, water, elevators, flying, bears, bats, audiences—these are just a few of the stimuli that evoke powerful fear responses, even phobias, in people. We can set up a fear response to a stimulus in seconds, and then we react with the same response each time the stimulus occurs. Yet there is a technique we can use to "unlearn" that fear response, no matter how long it has been operating. And, in most cases, the process takes less than an hour.

The technique—sometimes called "three-way dissociation"—is so powerful and so dependent on an experienced, sensitive friend or guide, that I almost decided not to include it in this book. In fact, I debated the issue for two years while completing the manuscript. What finally convinced me to write this chapter was the debilitating nature of strong fears. Another consideration was that the technique is being taught more widely, and a detailed printed version may be helpful.

There are many questions about why this unlearning process works. Perhaps it moves the stimulus-response learning to a different part of the brain and disconnects the fear part of the learning in the move. I do not know why this technique works, but I have seen its effectiveness again and again. You can "unlearn" fears—even fears that have existed for 10, 20, or 30 years.

During one of my negotiation seminars, a participant brought up his fear of flying. An executive in a holding company, Bob had to take business trips twice a month. He had taken an informal poll of his colleagues and found that two out of three were afraid of flying. Yet all these individuals spent many hours each month on airplanes.

Even as Bob was talking about flying, sweat had broken out on his forehead and above his lip. I asked, "Are you flying home tomorrow night?"

"Yes," he replied, taking out a handkerchief to wipe his face.

"Would you like to fix your fear of flying for good?"

He looked disbelieving but said "Sure."

I turned to the class and asked, "How many of you have a fear of flying?"

I was really surprised when all the people in the room raised their hands. I interrupted the class schedule and did an immediate group session on fear.

Fear is a learned response. The cure is to unlearn the response.

Fear of the unknown
and fear of flying are
unnecessary.

The only other time I interrupted a business semi-nar to deal with fear was at the World Trade Center in New York City. I was conducting a training seminar for Citibank on the fifty-fifth floor, and one person had turned pale as she first entered the classroom. The windows in the room stretched from floor to ceil-ing, with panoramic views of Manhattan. Madelyn was not enjoying the views. I said to her, "I notice you avoid looking out the windows. Is anything wrong?"

She replied through tight lips, "I don't like heights."

"Would you like to change that?" I asked.

"Could I?"

We were both almost whispering, as if fear were not to be discussed in a normal tone.

"Yes," I replied, and we did.

Some fears that cause problems in business:

Fear of—

questions	math
presentations	computers
flying	elevators
getting performance reviews	crowds
giving performance reviews	bridges
the opposite sex	heights
the number 13	

UNLEARNING A FEAR RESPONSE

The technique I used with both Bob and Madelyn has six basic steps:

1. Select a trusted friend to act as a guide.
2. Set up a safe cue-key.
3. Dissociate (watch the fear response in a movie).
4. Play out pictures and sounds (in a dissociated state) until the fear is gone.
5. Set up communication between your Fearful part and your Creative or Problem-Solving part.
6. Imagine a future situation without the fear.

I want to emphasize the importance of a trusted friend to serve as a responsible guide. Being safe is the key to this entire process. If you wish to challenge a fear, be sure to select a friend with whom you feel safe. No maybes. Someone you really trust.

It is essential to choose a quiet place where the two of you will not be interrupted as you go through this process. Erasing or "unlearning" fear digs deep into behaviors that are outside conscious control and, in so doing, places the person challenging his/her fear in unfamiliar internal states. These internal states are helpful in reorganizing fears and need to be dealt with in a sensitive, aware manner by the person acting as a guide. (Your guide should read the section "A Word to Guides" later in this chapter before s/he works with you on this technique.)

Mind games can cause extreme anxiety, but so, of course, do the fears. I think the advantages of reorganizing fears outweigh the disadvantages of temporary anxiety. But let me stress the importance of calling in a professional if the anxiety becomes too great to manage.

To reduce anxiety, set up a safe, secure cue-key before you begin this technique.

Erase Fears

I am going to give you a detailed version of the unlearning technique, but it can be shortened and modified, depending on the individuals who are working together. The important concepts and the sequence of steps on page 226 give you a structure for working creatively and flexibly. You can develop your own format around these steps. Remember, you are producing your own movie, so be as creative as you wish.

Here is a mnemonic to help you remember the process.

E   Establish a cue-key for a safe, secure place

R   Reseat yourself, in your imagination, in a movie theater

A   Ask your Creative part to run the movie projector

S   Start movie with scenes of stimulus and fear response

E   Expand movie to include sensory-based data (*see* and *hear* data only) pertaining to the fear

F   Film edit: arrange music, scene sequences; select colors or black and white; change speed—faster, slower, still frames, etc.

E   Envision movie made up of former fear situations

A   Ask your Creative part to join your younger self in the movie, and tell that self what you know now that you did not know then

R   Run movie until negative charge is gone

S   Step into future without the fear (future-pace)

As we go through the process in detail, let's assume you are the person who is working to unlearn a fear—you are the challenger—and the friend who is helping you is the guide.

Establish a cue-key for a safe, secure place. Your guide should be skillful in setting up a cue-key (explained in Chapter 11). The guide asks you to return to a specific past experience in which you felt safe and secure. You should see the place, hear the sounds of security, and feel safe and comfortable as you call up this one memory. At the height of the memory, your guide touches the back of your hand. After 1 or 2 minutes, the guide touches the spot again and asks you if the cue-key brings up the feeling of being safe and secure. If the answer is "yes" and the nonverbal information (facial expression, breathing, body posture) is congruent with "yes," then you may proceed to the next step. If the answer is "no," do not continue the process.

Reseat yourself, in your imagination, in a movie theater. Your guide asks you to imagine a movie theater in which you are the only one in the audience. Your guide waits, then asks if you can do this. If the answer is "yes," proceed. If the answer is "no," stop here. Do *not* use this technique.

Ask your Creative part to run the movie projector. Your guide asks you to allow your Creative part to float up to the projection booth to run the movie. If you are not sure you have a Creative part, try your Problem-Solving part.

Start movie with scenes of stimulus and fear response. Begin to select scenes for a movie about your fear. Your Creative part may choose to go immediately to the pivotal event that set up the fear, or it may select the most recent event that triggered the old response. The sequence is not important. Your Creative part continues to play the movie about the fear as long as scenes appear on the screen and there is any emotional charge left.

Expand movie to include sensory-based data (*see* and *hear* data only) pertaining to the fear. As the memory unfolds on the screen, you may recall long-forgotten pictures and sounds. These movie pictures and sounds may activate the fear, and if this occurs, your guide presses the safe cue-key. Your guide may wish to activate the safe cue-key all during the movie or may simply touch it when an emotional response calls for it.

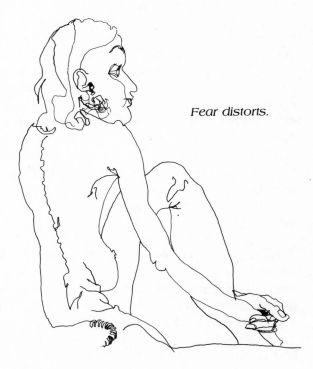

Fear distorts.

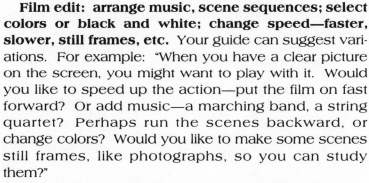

"You are safe. This is only pretend. This is not real. You are pretending to watch a movie."

The guide should be alert to any signs of fear or agitation in the challenger as the movie runs. In addition to activating the cue-key for safety and comfort, the guide can reassure the challenger verbally: "You are safe. We are pretending to watch a movie. This is not real. You are safe. You are comfortable. You are only pretending."

Film edit: arrange music, scene sequences; select colors or black and white; change speed—faster, slower, still frames, etc. Your guide can suggest variations. For example: "When you have a clear picture on the screen, you might want to play with it. Would you like to speed up the action—put the film on fast forward? Or add music—a marching band, a string quartet? Perhaps run the scenes backward, or change colors? Would you like to make some scenes still frames, like photographs, so you can study them?"

The guide should not rush this process. The challenger may take 10 to 30 minutes to play all the movie scenes. Once the emotional charge around the movie has diminished, the guide moves on to the next step.

Envision movie made up of former fear situations. When you feel safe, as a result of the cue-key, you will experience the pictures and sounds formerly associated with your fear response in a new way. You will find that the fear is no longer attached to these situations. The loss of fear seems to cause a change in neurology.

Ask your Creative part to join your younger self in the movie, and tell that self what you know now that you did not know then. Your guide suggests that your Creative part float down from the projection booth and join you in the audience. Then imagine your Creative part walking down the aisle and into the movie. As you watch your Creative part act in the movie, run whatever scenes seem appropriate. Then ask your Creative part to tell your younger self in the movie whatever learnings would be useful for that self to know. Your Creative part may want to give your younger self a hug, and reassure that self that s/he has an ally.

The guide can encourage communication between parts. For example: "Before you leave your younger self, you may want to tell him/her something that you have learned or unlearned. And remember, some fear is useful, so retain a realistic amount of fear to keep you safe. Have your Creative part decide how much fear is useful and when."

Run movie until negative charge is gone. When your guide senses that the emotional charge around the fear has dissipated, s/he suggests that your Creative part return to join you in the theater seat. Once your Creative part is back inside, you are ready for the last step.

Step into future without the fear (future-pace). To be sure the technique has worked, the guide asks you to project yourself forward in time and imagine a scene similar to one in which the fear would have occurred in the past. When the process has been successfully completed, only a slight fear will be present in the imaginary future scene.

Imagine a future without fear.

The guide should watch the challenger's responses to the future scene to determine whether the unlearning is complete. A giggle is a sure sign, and complete relaxation as the future movie runs is another good indicator.

Caution: Be sure and keep a *reasonable* amount of fear. Heights, bears, cliffs, snakes, and similar objects are somewhat dangerous, so a reasonable amount of fear is useful. This unlearning technique is so powerful that it can erase all fear, and some fear is necessary for survival.

If, for some reason, a strong fear is still present, you and your guide may need to return to step 2 (imagine yourself seated in a movie theater) and go through the steps again. (This is usually not necessary.)

Once you—the challenger—have completed the sequence, you should remain with your guide until your internal state feels normal. Do not rush out quickly and drive away. You may want to talk over what happened in the movie—or maybe not. At any rate, you should relax while your conscious mind integrates all the new learning (half an hour or more). Make sure you have regained a normal thinking/waking state before resuming regular tasks. Your guide can be a resource in bringing closure to this experience and in readying you for reentry into the everyday world.

My fears seem to be stored together. When I reduced my fear of skiing—through lessons—I also reduced other nuisance fears, such as fear of hecklers in seminars and fear of making a mistake.

A WORD TO GUIDES

You have a very special role in this unlearning process; your friend is trusting you to help him/her challenge a strong response that is disrupting and, possibly, painful. Because the internal states generated by this powerful technique may also be very strong, you should be alert to any extreme or problem reactions. For example:

Tears. If the challenger's tears last 10 minutes or less, that's fine. After 10 minutes, you should watch closely for signs of hysteria and activate the safe cue-key—even install new, more potent cue-keys if necessary. The challenger can call on resource states of calm, serene times in the past. You can choose words to help the challenger recall the pictures and sounds of these safe times, thus intensifying his/her feeling of safety and comfort.

Extreme agitation. If the challenger becomes extremely agitated and does not respond to his/her safe cue-key, stop the process. Set up a series of new, safe, comfort memories, establish skin cue-keys for these, and leave the challenger in a good emotional state. You may wish to try again, at another time, or the challenger may elect to seek professional help in dealing with his/her fear.

Shallow breathing. If the challenger begins to tighten up and his/her breathing becomes shallow, remind him/her to take deep breaths.

Deep reverie. Wait. Let the challenger proceed through each step at his/her own speed. You may wish to establish a signal—such as a nod—to indicate s/he has completed each stage of the process.

Inability to visualize clearly. Some people have difficulty seeing clear pictures on the screen, although they are able to imagine themselves in a theater seat, watching a movie. The technique will still work, as long as they can see *some* images. The guide may suggest ways to sharpen the movie scenes by asking questions. For example: "What are you wearing in that scene? What colors do you see? What season of the year is it? Do you remember any smells? Do you remember the people who were there? Can you hear any words or sounds?"

Remember to be creative and flexible within the basic format. Use the information in the six steps on page 226 in ways that will evoke the response you want. Some challengers like to see lots of subpersonalities in their movies; some, only one. Work with the challenger until s/he is fairly free of fear around the pivotal experience. Then be sure enough fear remains for a reasonable response to the stimulus.

Dissociation

Dissociation is a mental gymnastic that is useful for certain change techniques.

One-way dissociation: Watch a movie of your past.

Two-way dissociation: Sit in a theater and watch a movie of your past.

Three-way dissociation: Sit in a theater, watch a movie, and send your Creative self to the projection booth to select useful scenes.

CREATIVITY + FLEXIBILITY = SUCCESS

APPROPRIATE FEAR

The major concern I had in presenting this process is that it works too well. The challenger may erase all fear around the original stimulus, and that can be dangerous. I heard of one case in which this technique worked so well that a person who had been terrified of heights took up balancing on tenth-floor building parapets. So do not erase all fear. A little fear produces caution, which is useful with bears, snakes, cliffs, and so forth. Retain a reasonable amount of caution as you eliminate debilitating fear.

When I first learned this technique about eight years ago, I was skeptical. I had been trained in traditional as well as gestalt psychology, and I still believed Freud's admonition that deep change takes time—lots of time. As students, we practiced on each other with some surprising successes, but I was still skeptical. While attending a confluent education conference at the University of California at Santa Barbara, I decided to try the technique on a novice audience. At the conference, I put out a poster that said "Fear Erasure and Personal Change: 15 minutes, $1." (I donated the dollars to the group sponsoring the conference.)

I learned that people who pay $1 for personal change are more demanding than those who pay $100. I also learned that these fear-erasing techniques usually work. About 18 people signed up for 15 minutes. Their subjects ranged from bulimia to jealousy to fear of bears. Some subjects required more than 15 minutes, but we usually achieved insights and changes in less than an hour. For the bulimic graduate student, fear of rejection was the trigger. Jealousy has the same base fear. Erasing one student's extreme fear of bears was fun and took only 15 minutes.

Jealousy seems to be based on fear of rejection.

Paul and the Bears

My student was about 23 and handsome—Paul Bun-yan in a plaid shirt. So let's call him Paul. I was just playing around with new fear-erasing tech-niques, not taking any of this too seriously. When Paul said he had a bear phobia, I thought he had caught my playful mood and was pulling my leg. After 3 of the 15 minutes had elapsed, I realized he was very serious.

At that point, I asked, "Where do you find bears to be afraid of? Do you go to the zoo?"

Paul looked exasperated. "No, I go camping in the Sierra."

"Are there real bears in the Sierra?"

"You bet your buttons there are *real* bears."

"Oh, then if you have this bear fear, why do you go camping?"

"I've been going camping all my life. I love the wilderness. I just don't like bears, and since they come into the campsites at night, I never get any sleep."

"You stay awake all night?"

"All night."

"You don't close your eyes—even for 5 minutes?"

"Not even for 1 minute."

"How long do you usually camp out?"

"A week."

"That's a long time without sleep. We only have 7 more minutes. Let's get to work."

Working together, we were able to eliminate the extreme fear that had kept Paul sleepless while camping. A year later at the next conference, he said he had certainly been enjoying camping more, now that he could sleep.

One-Trial Learning

Fears of—bears, bridges, heights, rape, the dark, leaving the house, flying, driving, rats, spiders, snakes—keep people awake at night.

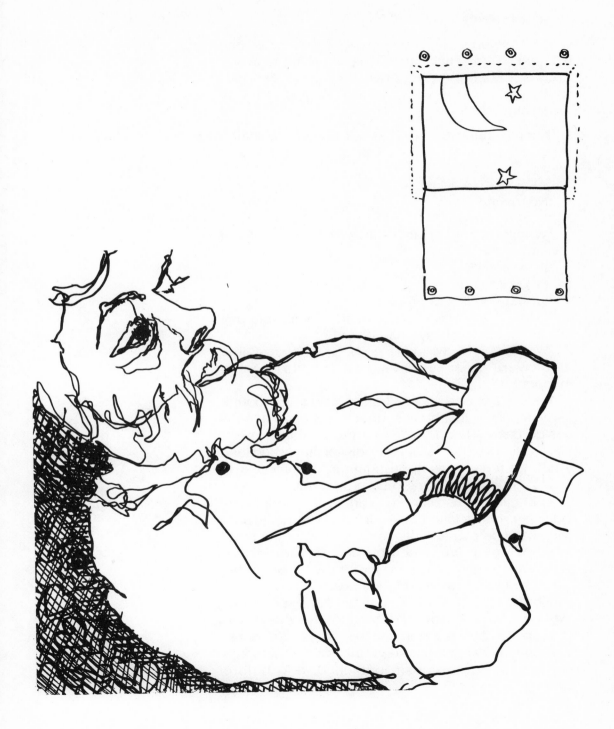

Near the Water

When I began to sell my seminars to business, one of my first potential clients was a training manager from Lockheed. He had never heard of neurolinguistics, but he was willing to give me an appointment.

After 15 minutes, we had not quite established rapport. Then he said something about his fear of water.

"All water?" I asked.

"No, rivers."

"Tell me about it."

"What's to tell? I have always been afraid of rivers."

"Do you swim?"

"Of course not."

"Would you like to erase your fear of water?"

"I don't think you can do anything with this particular fear. I've always had it, and I always will."

"Would you be willing to go back to the last time you were near a river and describe what happened?"

His eyes closed and he began telling me about a family reunion that had occurred a year ago at a riverside park. Then I guided him to an earlier memory. I did not use the theater dissociation because I did not feel it was appropriate in this context. I was a consultant calling on a new client.

This client was easy to work with. Simple, or one-way, dissociation was all that was necessary for him to be comfortably safe for most of the process. At one point, when he became somewhat anxious, I merely reminded him he was safe in his office, watching his own memories.

We finally got back to the pivotal experience. When he was 5 years old, he and his cousin had been playing on a log in shallow water. Suddenly the log was caught in a surge that swept them into deep water. His cousin panicked, and before

Some experts say there are only two emotions: love and fear. If the fear were erased, what would be left?

grown-ups could reach them, had grabbed him and pulled him under water. Until now, my client had had amnesia for the entire experience. Once he could remember being pulled out by his uncle, he no longer experienced the uncontrollable fear.

He opened his eyes, looked at me and said, "I think the YMCA gives swimming lessons year round."

After that, we certainly had rapport.

It is satisfying to be able to help people improve their lives by giving them new thinking skills and new options in behaviors. The worst thing about fears is that they limit you. They cause pain, yes, but the pain is slight compared to all the potential actions that are short-circuited by the fear. These truncated and inexperienced possibilities are a real tragedy.

Living your life without fear is a gift worth giving yourself.

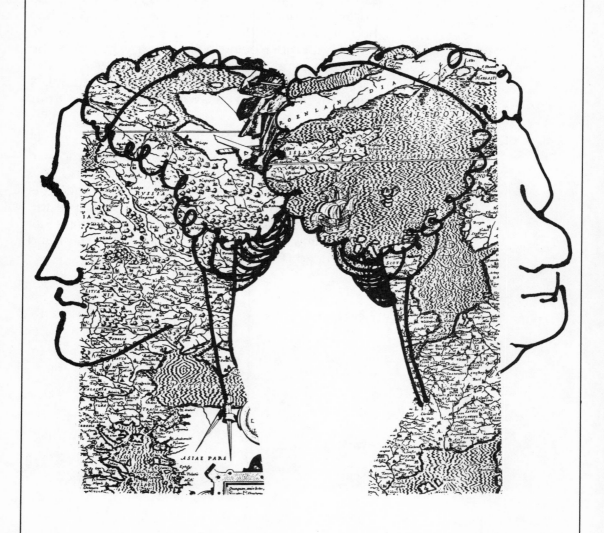

When we use our brains in creative ways to overlap realities, dovetailing becomes natural and almost inevitable. You have the tools you need for this creativity. You only need to open the toolbox.

Conclusion

When you know what you want and know you are not likely to get it unless the other person's energy is joined with yours, when you are sensitive to visual and auditory feedback and can incorporate this feedback into your ongoing language, then communication is a success, often a joy, sometimes a peak experience. At worst, communication becomes an intense challenge, calling on your deepest reservoirs of identity and purpose.

Maybe this is more than we should expect of the communication process, and maybe even more than you want. In that case, you have a choice. You can always lighten up—switch to small talk. However, many people seem to spend all their days in small talk. Connecting with another human being through words, facial expressions, body postures, and gestures has an inherent excitement and energy. Once you experience this type of communication, you recognize its value and seek it out.

Not all work interactions, of course, lend themselves to this kind of intensity. On the other hand, more and more people are aware that eight hours a day is a long time to spend in the barren desert of superficial communication. An oasis or two of meaningful connection with colleagues is almost a necessity for optimum performance. Also, the multifaceted cooperative setting necessary for a business group or a project team to work together successfully develops from real communication, not small talk. Infighting and hidden agendas can be eliminated by listening, by understanding, and by responding to the deep needs of others. Once you are in a resource state, your communication can be therapeutic.

As many of us have learned, a friend is often the best psychiatrist.

Conflicts appear to be almost inevitable when people work together, yet such conflicts can be resolved by recognizing that we each have a "correct" map of reality. Business conflicts—which cost thousands, perhaps millions, in lost revenues each month—can be resolved fairly easily, once we are willing to explore the other person's map with the intent of overlapping. Holding tight to your own map will get you a strong sense of being "right" and little else. If you wish to live in peace with your colleagues, and at the same time be successful in business, you will explore overlapping maps in creative ways and dovetail.

The process skills presented in this book will enable you to fine-tune your brain so that your day will contain satisfaction, purpose, and actualization of your own potential. People who know process skills, who can perceive the real meaning of verbal and nonverbal messages in a communication, and who can recognize when processes are changing, can respond appropriately. Companies that value people as their greatest asset and encourage their people to learn process skills will continue to respond in not only appropriate but optimum ways to a changing environment. These companies will survive the global competition and economic environment of the 1990s.

Be aware that each of us is more powerful and has more impact than we suspect. Using this personal power in a positive way during our business interactions can have corporate, city, state, perhaps national and global repercussions. Many people have already discovered their personal power, and use it daily. When you join them, you will find your energy moving to new levels, your interactions more satisfying, and your work more meaningful. I wish this for each of you.

Te—being in the right place, in the right frame of mind, at the right time—depends on you. The skills—and the choice—are now yours.

Epilogue

Here's a metaphor I want to leave you with. I heard it first from Leslie Cameron-Bandler. Thanks, Leslie.

Long ago in a faraway land, a teacher wanted to retire. During a lifetime of teaching, he had attracted many followers. He felt he owed them a successor—someone to carry on his work.

He had taught each day on the gentle slope of a mountain with a snowy peak. He sat near the middle of the slope, on a dais under a canopy, for the sun was often hot. His students would come and sit on the grass below the dais.

On this day, the teacher looked out at several students with the idea of choosing his successor. Finally, he left the dais and went out into the audience. Tapping one student on the shoulder, the teacher beckoned him to follow. He had chosen the one student who was always on time, always paid attention, usually asked a lot of questions, and seemed a good choice.

The student followed his master up onto the dais. His bearing was different from usual as he walked up the slope. He walked proudly—a bit too proudly. When he looked down at the students, his expression was full of satisfaction at being chosen. The master waited. The student then looked at the canopy overhead. Behind the canopy, hidden from the class, was an enormous machine like a giant ticker tape with a message on it that read, "Ask any question you wish, and I will answer."

The student's face fell. He looked at the master with disappointment and dismay. All along, he had never questioned his belief that the master had all the answers. Now he suddenly realized that a machine had been supplying the answers. The master noted his expression and signaled him to return to the grassy slope.

The next morning the master selected another student to sit with him on the dais. This student did not seem proud; in fact, he seemed almost too humble. The sight of the machine rendered him speechless. The master reluctantly sent him down the slope.

On the third morning, the master thought to himself, "A lifetime of teaching, and who has learned the most basic lessons?" He was very tired and discouraged. He looked over the students once more and finally went down to tap the shoulder of a rebellious, out-of-line, daydreaming newcomer—a student who asked impertinent questions, arrived late, left early, and always seemed surprised to find himself on the grassy slope.

This student walked up to the dais with an extremely curious look on his face. His walk was the same walk he used every day. He sat down under the canopy, looked at his teacher long and seriously, and then glanced up. At the sight of the message on the machine, he broke into a broad smile, took a breath, and said, "What question has my master never asked?"

With that, the master disappeared.

APPENDIX

A Parts Party

I was first introduced to the concept of Parts Party at Esalen Institute in the early seventies. Several seminar leaders used the idea in different ways, and I assumed that the technique had evolved from Fritz Perls's work in gestalt psychology. A colleague thought Virginia Satir was the creator of the Parts Party. I like to know the origins of good mental techniques, but I have not yet been able to trace this one to its source. In any event, my thanks to the person or group who created this useful and illuminating technique.

Some of you may already know about the Parts Party, and I gave an example in *Influencing with Integrity*. This concept is so central to knowing ourselves and so vital to achieving congruence that I want to outline it briefly here again. I use this technique in new conflict situations, and I am constantly surprised by what I learn.

First, choose a time when you can be undisturbed for an hour or so. Next, make a list of all the parts of your personality that want to be heard on a specific issue. Here is one of my lists, derived from a comfort/challenge conflict I have. This basic dichotomy shows up again and again in my behavior—much as your dichotomies show up in your behaviors.

Comfort Parts
Dr. Security, Ph.D.
Mrs. Thrift

Challenge Parts
Ms. New Experiences
Ms. Risk
Miss Money Unimportant

Nonaligned Parts
Ms. Nondirected Creative
Ms. Flow/Wastetime

The agenda for this Parts Party is to decide how much of my money and my workday to allot to the new marketing company I was creating. Should I invest my last nickel, or should I hold some money back in case the company fails? As for work time, even though time is limited, we all "waste" some of it. Knowing how much to waste and how to allocate the rest of your time is very useful in developing congruent behavior at work.

For this party, I decided that the invited parts needed to discuss exactly how much money and how much of my work time I should spend on being comfortable, how much to spend on being challenged, and how much to "waste."

I decided to create a new part to be Conflict Manager. ("Who is in charge?" is a question you will have to decide for yourself. You can choose an old part you trust, or create a new one.)

I called the meeting to order in my dining room, after locking all the doors. I then imagined each part sitting in an elegant, turn-of-the-century boardroom full of massive antique furniture—a boardroom left over from a former age, when you climbed the ladder of success and stayed on top. Looking around, I thought, "My subpersonalities are a strange-looking group. I'm glad no one else is here to see them. Listen, they are already arguing."

Dr. Security, Ph.D., dressed in a dark blue wool suit, a white shirt, and low heels, was talking loudly, as though she were afraid she would not be allowed the floor for long. "No more risks. Do not risk any money at all. Stick to what works. Genie is safe as long as she continues to do what she's been doing. No changes."

Ms. Risk, remarkable for her décolletage, interrupted, "Boring, boring, boring. You are boring. Your ideas are nonmotivational. Why get up in the morning if you are going to do the same old safe thing hour after hour? I need all Genie's money, and all she can borrow, and I need at least 80 percent of her workday for risky enterprises. If we go under, she'll find a way out."

Conflict Manager commented, "We have two opposing viewpoints. Who else wants to be heard?"

"I'm with Dr. Security," Mrs. Thrift said, jumping in. "Genie has no extra money to gamble, and we need 100 percent of her time just to keep us safe." Mrs. Thrift had on a limp suit that was at least ten years old and shiny across the rump.

"I'm joining Ms. Risk," announces Ms. New Experiences. "But together we must have 100 percent of money and time—not just 80 percent. Got to keep her motivated." Her purple, green, and orange sweater draped dramatically over her striped tights.

"That's 200 percent," Conflict Manager was adding figures thoughtfully. "Let's be reasonable. We have only 100 percent available."

Ms. Nondirected Creative threw off her academic robe, showing off her bikini, and said, "You need my help, Conflict Manager. All you are doing is stating the obvious. You need new thinking skills, new approaches. I think I have an ally in Ms. Flow/Wastetime. If you will give us a moment to caucus, I think we can come up with a solution."

Ms. Flow/Wastetime, in a surprised voice, chimed in, "I didn't know you felt that way about me, Nondirected/Creative, but thanks for your support. Yes, I think we can solve this. With 7 parts here all wanting 100 percent of her time, maybe we can flow right into a creative way to divide 7 into 100 percent. Or is it 100 percent into 7? I never can remember." Ms. Flow/Wastetime had on a white chiffon something that fluttered with every breeze.

Dr. Security hit the table with the palm of her hand, and everyone jumped. "She needs to succeed; succeeding means security. No more risks. No more quarter-million-dollar videos—no matter how creative she's feeling. That's an expensive medium. Let's focus on money. I'm sure Mrs. Thrift agrees. She's a sensible person."

Miss Money Unimportant shrugged her shoulders. "I couldn't disagree more."

Conflict Manager looked pained and said, "But 700 percent is not available. The only sensible suggestion I've heard so far is from Ms. Nondirected/Creative. How much time do you need to caucus?"

"Five minutes."

"Good. Let's do it," said Conflict Manager.

Five minutes later Ms. Nondirected/Creative and Ms. Flow/Wastetime announced their plan: "Genie can spend 60 percent of her workday selling videos, and she can spend 100 percent of her money—but no borrowing. This plan will produce money for Mrs. Thrift and safety for Dr. Security. Selling is full of new experiences and often risky, so this plan should also satisfy you two," nodding to Ms. New Experiences and Ms. Risk. "Miss Money Unimportant will go along with 100 percent of the money, won't you? Then the remaining 40 percent of the time can be used by my partner and me. We'll keep Genie motivated, free from tension, and full of energy."

In the end, all agreed to the proposal from Ms. Non-directed/Creative and Ms. Flow/Wastetime, as offensive as it was. Dr. Security and Mrs. Thrift finally agreed when it was pointed out that selling opened up opportunities for new income and that creative endeavors were what started the business in the first place.

Now a quick review of how to conduct your own Parts Party:

1. Make a list of major parts
2. Draw up the agenda
3. Call a meeting
4. Name a Conflict Manager
5. Negotiate and agree

If you discover from all these discussions and exercises that you have many subpersonalities struggling to express themselves, rejoice. You have depth. You are interesting. You are complex.

Glossary

As if technique—A method for achieving an outcome by pretending it has already happened.

Auditories—People who primarily use their ears to perceive the world and who depend on spoken words or sounds for the information that determines their behavior.

Brainstorming—A technique for breaking out of your usual thought patterns into creative thinking.

Change history technique—A series of mental steps to change memories that have continuing negative impact to memories with a positive or even numinous influence.

Cognitive learning—A complex series of neurological responses involving several different parts of the brain and associations to these responses, which become stabilized.

Conflicts—Misunderstandings in communication that result from noncreative thinking patterns.

Congruence—A unified, unimpaired state; when all a person's parts work together toward his/her outcome.

Creative problem-solving—A four-step process:
  1. Clarifying your desired state in sensory-based terms
  2. Brainstorming
  3. Using judgment for prioritizing possible courses of action
  4. Implementing with feedback at checkpoints

Cue-key—A stimulus that has been deliberately associated with a specific response or responses.

Dissociated state—A technique for experiencing certain moments or memories while deleting specific sensory data.

Dovetailing—Fitting together to form a union; matching outcomes to achieve a win/win+ solution through creative problem-solving.

Ecology—The relationship between organisms and their environment.

Energy—1. Vigor or power in action. 2. Vitality and intensity of expression. 3. The capacity for action or accomplishment. 4. Activity. 5. Capacity for work.

Engram—A stabilized neurological pattern.

Essence—A person's intrinsic nature; one's heart of hearts; the real you, as opposed to the roles you play.

Eye accessing cues—The eye movements that indicate a person is using pictures, sounds, or feelings to "make sense" of the world and to remember past experiences.

Flexibility—Having more than one choice of behavior in a situation.

Fluff—The unimportant words that are used to hide the nuggets of real needs and desires in communication.

Generalization—The brain process by which we draw inferences or categorize from particulars to universal applications.

Gestalt psychology—The discipline that evolved from the study of perceptions, needs, belief systems, and their impact on human behavior.

Habit learning—A form of stimulus-response that is simpler than cognitive learning and that becomes stabilized. Habit learning uses shorter circuitry and fewer components than complex learning.

Identification—A mental process by which we associate ourselves closely with someone else in order to match and acquire their characteristics.

Integrity—State of being complete, undivided, and unimpaired, as well as honest.

Internal state—The emotional climate predominant in one's awareness at any one moment in time.

Introjection—The process of acquiring introjects.

Introjects—Unconscious rules that control behavior.

Key words and phrases—The important verbal components of the communication process.

Kinesthetics—People who "feel" their way through their experiences. Kinesthetics sort both external and internal stimuli through their feelings, and they use their feelings to make their life decisions.

Left-brain skills—Language and logical, analytic, sequential thinking are considered to be left-brain skills.

Linguistics—The study of the nature and structure of human speech.

Map of reality—Each person's representation of the universe based on his/her individual perceptions and experiences.

Marqueeing—Establishing a planned response to a specific stimulus or cue-key. In neurolinguistic programming, this is called anchoring.

Metaphor—A simple or complex comparison of unlike objects or situations, with intrinsic elements analogous to a present state and also to a desired outcome.

Modal operators—A linguistic term for rules ("shoulds," "can'ts," etc.).

Negative communication—Any interaction that leaves either party in a less than resourceful state (i.e., feeling depressed, inadequate, guilty, drained).

Neurolinguistic programming—A discipline based on the idea that neurology, language, and behavior are interrelated and can be changed by specific interventions; based on studies of masters in several fields.

Neurolinguistics—The study of language, neurology, and human behavior and their interactions.

One down—That mental state in which you act as if you are less smart, less talented, or less successful than your communication partner.

One up—That mental state in which you act as if you are better, smarter, or more successful than your communication partner.

Outcome—A specific, positive, sensory-based desired result.

Paralinguistics—The discipline that concerns itself with all aspects of communication—the context or setting of the interaction, the nonverbal communication, and so forth.

Parts—*See* Subpersonality.

Pattern—A neurological response that has the potential of habituation or is already stabilized.

Pattern-interrupt—Breaking a neurological pattern before completion.

PEGASUS—An acronym for specific meeting procedures that will shorten meeting time and provide high-quality outcomes.

Perceptions—Information gathered by one or more of the senses and processed by the brain.

Personality—The dynamic psyche that constitutes

and animates the individual and makes his/her experience of life unique.

Polarities—Subpersonalities with opposite characteristics (e.g., good boy–bad boy).

Positive communication—Any interaction that leaves all participants energized, feeling resourceful, appreciated, and validated for their contributions.

Process skills—The ability to recognize and respond to the underlying meaning of both verbal and nonverbal messages in a communication.

Rapport—A process of establishing and maintaining a relationship of mutual trust and understanding between two or more parties; in business, rapport includes trust in another's competence for the task at hand.

Reframing—A technique for changing one's perspective so that new options are perceived.

Resource state—The sensory experience associated with a time when a person felt confident, energized, and competent.

Right-brain skills—Recognition of faces and voices, spatial discrimination, pattern recognition, and holistic all-at-one-time insights are thought to be right-brain skills.

Scramble—A technique for mixing negative and positive experiences until the positive experience wins as a trigger for the current internal state.

Sensory acuity—The ability to hear more and see more than the average person.

Sensory-based—Relating to what a person sees, hears, feels, tastes, and smells.

Sensory data—The pictures, feelings, sounds, smells, and tastes that create our reality and our memories.

Stimulus-response—An association between an experience and a subsequent reaction; the natural learning process Ivan Pavlov demonstrated when he hooked the ringing of a bell to saliva secretion in dogs.

Stimulus-response learning—Stabilizing a neurological response or responses so that appropriate input into the circuitry will recall the same response. Sometimes used to include associations to the responses as well.

Stimulus-response pattern (stimulus-response plus associations)—Stabilizing a neurological response or responses, plus associations, so that appropriate input into the circuitry will recall the same response.

Strategy—A thinking process with a purpose; often has a decision component that is a comparison in order to make a choice.

Subpersonality—A well-developed pattern of responses clustered around one or more behaviors that are consistent in their appearance when activated by specific stimuli.

Switching marquees—A technique for changing negative responses to positive responses at the neurological level.

Synergy—The action of two or more organisms combined to achieve an effect of which each is individually incapable.

Syntonics—The discipline of effective business communication, based on the principles and skills of neurolinguistics, gestalt psychology, and systems theory.

VAKOG—Acronym for visual, auditory, kinesthetic, olfactory, and gustatory; the sensory data we use to store our experiences as memories.

Visuals—People who primarily use their eyes to perceive the world and who trust their images as a basis for decisions.

Bibliography

ANATOMY, PHYSIOLOGY, AND NEUROLOGY

Calvin, William H., and George A. Ojemann. *Inside the Brain.* New York: New American Library, 1980.

Eccles, J. C. *Facing Reality.* New York: Springer Verlag, 1970.

Eccles, J. C., and Daniel N. Robinson. *The Wonder of Being Human: Our Brain and Our Mind.* Boston: New Science Library, 1985.

Diagram Group. *The Brain, A User's Manual.* New York: G. P. Putnam's Sons, 1982.

Hecaen, Henry, and Martin L. Albert. *Human Neuropsychology.* Melbourne, Florida: Robert E. Krieger, 1986.

Heilman, Kenneth M., and Edward Valenstein, eds. *Clinical Neuropsychology.* New York: Oxford University Press, 1985.

Lashley, K. S. *The Neuropsychology of Lashley.* New York: McGraw-Hill, 1960.

Mesulam, M. M., ed. *Principles of Behavioral Neurology.* Philadelphia: Davis, 1985.

Mitchell, G. A. G. *The Essentials of Neuroanatomy.* Edinburgh: Churchill Livingstone, 1971.

Ornstein, Robert, and Richard F. Thompson. *The Amazing Brain.* Boston: Houghton Mifflin, 1984.

Sherrington, C. S. *Man on His Nature.* London: Cambridge University Press, 1940.

BRAIN SKILLS

Adams, James L. *Conceptual Blockbusting: A Guide to Better Ideas.* New York: W. W. Norton, 1974.

de Bono, Edward. *de Bono's Thinking Course.* New York: Facts on File Publications, 1982.

———. *The Happiness Purpose.* Middlesex, England: Penguin Books, 1979.

———. *Lateral Thinking: Creativity Step by Step.* New York: Harper and Row, 1970.

———. *New Think.* New York: Avon Books, 1967.

———. *Opportunities.* Middlesex, England: Penguin Books, 1980.

———. *PO: Beyond Yes and No.* Middlesex, England: Penguin Books, 1973.

McKim, Robert. *Experiences in Visual Thinking.* Monterey, Calif.: Brooks/Cole, 1972.

Smith, Adam. *Powers of Mind.* New York: Ballantine Books, 1975.

BUSINESS

Blanchard, Kenneth, and Spencer Johnson. *The One-Minute Manager.* New York: William Morrow, 1982.

Brandt, Steven C. *Entrepreneuring.* Reading, Mass.: Addison-Wesley, 1982.

Cooper, Ken. *Body Business.* New York: Amacom, 1979.

Crosby, Philip B. *The Art of Getting Your Own Sweet Way.* New York: McGraw-Hill, 1982.

Deal, Terrence E., and Alan Kennedy. *Corporate Cultures.* Reading, Mass.: Addison-Wesley, 1982.

de Bono, Edward. *Six Thinking Hats: An Essential Approach to Business Management.* Boston: Little, Brown, 1985.

———. *Tactics: The Art and Science of Success.* Boston: Little, Brown, 1984.

Drucker, Peter F. *The Changing World of the Executive.* New York: Truman Talley Books, 1982.

———. *Concept of the Corporation,* 2nd ed. New York: Mentor Books, 1983.

———. *The Effective Executive.* London: Heineman, 1967.

———. *Management Tasks, Responsibilities, Practices.* New York: Harper and Row, 1973.

———. *People and Performance: The Best of Peter Drucker on Management.* New York: Harper and Row, 1977.

Dyer, William G. *Team Building: Issues and Alternatives.* Reading, Mass.: Addison-Wesley, 1977.

Greiner, Larry, and Robert O. Metzger. *Consulting to Management.* Englewood Cliffs, N.J.: Prentice-Hall, 1983.

Huseman, R., M. Lahiff, and J. D. Hatfield. *Business Communication: Strategies and Skills.* Hinsdale, Illinois: Dryden Press, 1981.

Katz, D., and R. Kahn. *The Social Psychology of Organizations,* 2nd ed. New York: Wiley, 1978.

Laborde, Genie Z. *Influencing with Integrity: Management Skills for Communication and Negotiation.* Palo Alto, Calif.: Syntony, 1984.

————. "Productive Policies—Business Procedures Which Reflect the Bank's Personality in the Marketplace." *The Southern Banker,* May 1984.

Levinson, Harry. *Executive.* Cambridge, Mass.: Harvard University Press, 1968.

————. "Gut Feelings Are Still the Basis for Executive Decisions." *Levinson Letter,* July 15, 1977.

Mager, Robert F., and Peter Pipe. *Analyzing Performance Problems.* Belmont, Calif.: Pitman Learning, 1970.

McCarthy, John J. *Why Managers Fail . . . and What to Do About It,* 2nd ed. New York: McGraw-Hill, 1978.

Munter, Mary. *Guide to Managerial Communication.* Englewood Cliffs, N.J.: Prentice-Hall, 1982.

Naisbitt, John, and Patricia Aburdene. *Reinventing the Corporation: Transforming Your Job and Your Company for the Information Society.* New York: Warner Books, 1985.

Peters, Thomas J., and Robert H. Waterman, Jr. *In Search of Excellence: Lessons from America's Best Run Companies.* New York: Harper and Row, 1982.

Williams, Frederick. *Executive Communication Power: Basic Skills for Management Success.* Englewood Cliffs, N.J.: Prentice-Hall, 1983.

EDUCATION

Averch, Harvey, et al. *How Effective Is Schooling? A Critical Review and Synthesis of Research Findings.* Final Report to the President's Commission on School Finance. Santa Monica, Calif.: Rand Corporation, 1971.

Bandura, Albert, and Robert Jerry. "Role of Symbolic Coding and Rehearsal Processes in Observational

Learning." *Journal of Personality and Social Psychology*, vol. 26, no. 1, 1973.

Brown, George I. *Human Teaching for Human Learning: An Introduction to Confluent Education.* New York: Viking, 1971.

————, ed. *The Live Classroom: Innovation Through Confluent Education and Gestalt.* New York: Viking, 1975.

Brown, George I., with Mark Phillips and Stewart Shapiro. *Getting It All Together: Confluent Education.* Bloomington, Indiana: Phi Beta Kappa Educational Foundation, 1976.

LINGUISTICS

Birdwhistell, Ray L. *Kinesics and Context: Essays on Body Motion Communication.* Philadelphia: University of Pennsylvania Press, 1970.

Hall, Edward T. *The Silent Language.* Garden City, N.Y.: Doubleday, 1973.

MISCELLANEOUS

Bach, Richard. *Illusions.* New York: Dell, 1977.

Castaneda, Carlos. *Tales of Power.* New York: Simon and Schuster, 1974.

Grinder, John T., and S. H. Elgin. *A Guide to Transformational Grammar: History, Theory, Practice.* New York: Holt, Rinehart & Winston, 1973.

Heinlein, Robert A. *Stranger in a Strange Land.* New York: Berkeley Publishing, 1968.

Laborde, Genie Z., and Hazel Beatrous. *Tranquilizers for His Cup.* New York: Doubleday, 1961.

Machlin, Evangeline. *Speech for the Stage.* New York: Theatre Arts Books, 1980.

NEGOTIATION

Calero, Henry, and Bob Oskam. *Negotiate the Deal You Want.* New York: Dodd, Mead, 1983.

Fisher, Roger, and William Ury. *Getting to Yes.* Boston: Houghton Mifflin, 1981.

Huthwaite Research Group Limited. *The Behavior of Successful Negotiators.* London: 1976/78.

Nierenberg, Gerard I. *Fundamentals of Negotiating.* New York: Hawthorn Books, 1973.

Raiffa, Howard. *The Art and Science of Negotiation.* Cambridge, Mass.: Harvard University Press, 1982.

NEUROLINGUISTICS

Bailey, Rodger. "Neurolinguistics: Information Processing in the Human Biocomputer." *J C Penney Forum,* November 1982.

Bandler, Richard, and John Grinder. *Frogs into Princes.* Moab, Utah: Real People Press, 1979.

———. *Patterns of the Hypnotic Techniques of Milton H. Erickson, M.D.,* vol. 1. Cupertino, Calif.: Meta Publications, 1976.

———. *Reframing.* Moab, Utah: Real People Press, 1982.

———. *The Structure of Magic,* vols. 1 and 2. Palo Alto, Calif.: Science and Behavior Books, 1975 and 1976.

Bandler, Richard, John Grinder, and Virginia Satir. *Changing with Families.* Palo Alto, Calif.: Science and Behavior Books, 1976.

———. *Solutions* (formerly, *They Lived Happily Ever After*). San Rafael, Calif.: FuturePace, 1985.

DeLozier, Judith, and John Grinder. *Turtles All the Way Down.* Santa Cruz, Calif.: Grinder, DeLozier and Associates, 1987.

Dilts, Robert. "Let NLP Work for You." *Real Estate Today,* February 1982.

Dilts, Robert, Leslie Cameron-Bandler, Richard Bandler, John Grinder, and Judith DeLozier. *Neuro-Linguistic Programming,* vol. 1. Cupertino, Calif.: Meta Publications, 1980.

Douglis, Carole. "The Beat Goes On." *Psychology Today,* November 1987.

Farrelly, Frank, and Jeff Brandsma. *Provocative Therapy.* Cupertino, Calif.: Meta Publications, 1978.

Goleman, Daniel. "People Who Read People." *Psychology Today,* July 1979.

Gordon, David. *Therapeutic Metaphors.* Cupertino, Calif.: Meta Publications, 1978.

Gordon, David, and Maribeth Meyers-Anderson. *Phoenix: Therapeutic Techniques of Milton H. Erickson, M.D.* Cupertino, Calif.: Meta Publications, 1981.

Grinder, John, and Richard Bandler. *The Structure of Magic,* vol. 2. Palo Alto, Calif.: Science and Behavior Books, 1976.

———. *Trance-Formations.* Moab, Utah: Real People Press, 1981.

Laborde, Genie Z. "Don't Eat the Menu." *New Realities,* vol. IV, no. 4, December 1981.

———. "Neuro-linguistic Programming." *New Realities,* vol. IV, no. 1, April 1981.

———. "Neurolinguistics: Reading Between the Lines." *Real Estate Business,* Spring 1985.

Laborde, Genie Z., and Bruce Dillman. "The Structure of Charisma: Playing with Power and Matches." *New Realities,* vol. IV, no. 4, December 1981.

Lankton, Steve. *Practical Magic.* Cupertino, Calif.: Meta Publications, 1979.

Maron, Davida. "Neurolinguistic Programming: The Answer to Change?" *Training and Development Journal,* October 1979.

McCaskey, Michael B. "The Hidden Messages Managers Send." *Harvard Business Review,* November/December 1979.

Moine, Donald J. "A Psycholinguistic Study of the Patterns of Persuasion Used by Successful Salespeople." Dissertation, University of Oregon, 1981. Ann Arbor, Mich.: University Microfilms International, 1982.

Zientara, Marguerite. "IBMer Tells How to Handle a Primadonna." *Computerworld,* November 15, 1982.

PHILOSOPHY

Buber, Martin. *The Way of Man.* Secaucus, N.J.: Citadel, 1973.

Brugh, Joy. *Joy's Way.* Los Angeles: J. P. Tarcher, 1979.

Field, Reshad. *Steps to Freedom.* Putney, Vermont: Threshold Books, 1983.

Fromm, Erich. *The Art of Loving.* New York: Harper and Row, 1956.

Fuller, Buckminister. *I Seem to Be a Verb.* New York: Bantam, 1970.

Hoff, Benjamin. *The Tao of Pooh.* Middlesex, England: Penguin Books, 1983.

Mishkin, Mortimer, and Tim Appenzeller. "The Anatomy of Memory." *Scientific American,* June 1987.

Moss, Richard. *The Black Butterfly: Western Approaches to Personal Growth.* Boston: New Science Library, 1981.

———. *Up from Eden: A Transpersonal View of Human Evolution.* Garden City, N.Y.: Anchor Press/Doubleday, 1981.

Wing, R. L., trans. *The Tao of Power: Lao Tzu's Classic Guide to Leadership, Influence, and Excellence.* Garden City, N.Y.: Doubleday, 1986.

PSYCHOLOGY

Assagioli, Roberto. *Psychosynthesis.* New York: Viking, 1971.

Auerswald, Edgar. "Thinking About Thinking About Mental Health." In *American Handbook of Psychiatry,* vol. 2, 2nd ed. Gerald Caplans, ed. New York: Basic Books, 1974.

Barron, Frank. *The Shaping of Personality: Conflict, Choice and Growth.* New York: Harper and Row, 1979.

Baumgardner, Patricia. *Legacy from Fritz.* Palo Alto, Calif.: Science and Behavior Books, 1975.

Bentov, Itzhak. *Stalking the Wild Pendulum: On the Mechanics of Consciousness.* New York: Bantam Books, 1977.

Berelson, Bernard, and Gary Steiner. *Human Behavior: An Inventory of Scientific Findings.* New York: Harcourt Brace and World, 1964.

Bialer, I. "Conceptualization of Success and Failure in Mentally Retarded and Normal Children." *Journal of Personality,* vol. 29, 1961.

Brown, Judith R. *Back to the Beanstalk.* La Jolla, Calif.: Psychology and Consulting Associates Press, 1979.

Crandall, V. C., W. Katkovsky, and V. J. Crandall. "Children's Belief in Their Control of Reinforcement in Intellectual-Academic Achievement Situations." *Child Development,* vol. 36, 1965.

Dement, William. *Some Must Watch While Some Must Sleep.* San Francisco: W. H. Freeman, 1972.

Downing, Jack. *Gestalt Awareness: Papers from the San Francisco Gestalt Institute.* New York: Harper and Row, 1976.

Downing, Jack, and Robert Marmorstein, eds. *Dreams and Nightmares.* New York: Harper and Row, 1973.

Enright, John. *Enlightening Gestalt: Waking Up from the Nightmare.* Mill Valley, Calif.: Pro Telos, 1980.

Fagan, Joen, and Irma Shepherd, eds. *Gestalt Therapy Now.* New York: Harper Colophon Books, 1970.

Freud, Sigmund. *Beyond the Pleasure Principle.* London: International Psycho-Analytical Press, 1922.

————. *Civilization and Its Discontents.* London: Hogarth Press and the Institute of Psycho-Analysis, 1973.

————. *The Ego and the Id.* London: Hogarth Press, 1957.

————. *The Future of an Illusion.* Garden City, N.Y.: Anchor Books, 1957.

————. *Group Psychology and the Analysis of the Ego.* New York: Liveright, 1951.

————. *Moses and Monotheism.* New York: Vintage Books, 1939.

————. *New Introductory Lectures on Psycho-Analysis.* London: Hogarth Press, 1974.

————. *On the Interpretation of Dreams.* London: George Allen and Unwin, 1954.

———. *An Outline of Psycho-Analysis.* New York: W. W. Norton, 1949.

———. *The Question of Lay Analysis.* London: Imago Publishing, 1947.

———. *Totem and Taboo.* New York: Vintage Books, 1946.

Gaines, Jack. *Fritz Perls Here and Now.* Millbrae, Calif.: Celestial Arts, 1979.

Hampden-Turner, Charles. *Maps of the Mind.* New York: Macmillan, 1981.

Huxley, Laura Archera. *You Are Not the Target.* North Hollywood, Calif.: Wilshire Book, 1972.

Janov, Arthur. *The Primal Scream.* New York: Dell, 1971.

Jones, Ernest. *Papers on Psycho-Analysis.* London: Bailliere, Tindall and Cox, 1950.

Jung, C. G. *Man and His Symbols.* New York: Dell, 1964.

———. *Modern Man in Search of a Soul.* New York: Harcourt, Brace and World, 1933.

———. *The Portable Jung.* New York: Penguin, 1976.

———. *Psyche and Symbol.* Garden City, N.Y.: Anchor Books/Doubleday, 1958.

———. *The Undiscovered Self.* New York: New American Library, 1957.

Klein, Melanie, P. Hermann, and R. E. Money-Kyrle, eds. *New Horizons in Psycho-Analysis.* New York: Basic Books, 1955.

Laborde, Genie Z. "Comparing Certain Theories and Therapies of Freud and Perls." *Gestalt Journal,* Spring 1979.

———. "An Exploration into the Practicability of Using Confluent Approaches in Increasing Awareness of

Introjects." Doctoral dissertation, University of California at Santa Barbara, 1976.

Laborde, Genie Z., and George I. Brown. "Introjects and Their Relationship to Locus of Control." *Integrative Therapie,* January 1981.

Laing, R. D. *The Divided Self.* New York: Pantheon Books, 1969.

———. *The Politics of Experience.* New York: Balantine Books, 1968.

———. *Self and Others.* New York: Penguin Books, 1972.

Laing, R. D., and A. Esterson. *Sanity, Madness and the Family.* New York: Penguin Books, 1970.

Lawrence, D. H. *Psychoanalysis and the Unconscious: Fantasia of the Unconscious.* New York: Viking, 1921.

Lichtenstein, E., and W. Craine. "The Importance of Subjective Evaluation of Reinforcement in Verbal Conditioning." *Journal of Experimental Research in Personality,* vol. 3, 1969.

Lilly, John C. *Programming and Metaprogramming in the Human Biocomputer.* New York: Bantam, 1972.

Maslow, Abraham. *Toward a Psychology of Being.* New York: Van Nostrand Reinhold, 1968.

McClain, E. W., and H. B. Andrews. "Self-Actualization Among Extremely Superior Students." *Journal of College Student Personnel,* 1972.

Meissner, W. W. "Notes on Identification III: The Concept of Identification." *Psycho-Analytic Quarterly,* vol. 41, 1972.

Menninger, Karl. *The Human Mind.* New York: Knopf, 1937.

———. *A Psychiatrist's World.* New York: Knopf, 1937.

Moustakas, Clark E. *Loneliness and Love.* Englewood Cliffs, N.J.: Prentice-Hall, 1972.

Ornstein, Robert E., ed. *The Nature of Human Consciousness.* New York: Viking, 1974.

Perls, Frederick. *Ego, Hunger, and Aggression.* New York: Vintage Books, 1967.

————. *The Gestalt Approach and Eye-Witness to Therapy.* Palo Alto, Calif.: Science and Behavior Books, 1973.

————. *Gestalt Therapy Verbatim.* Toronto: Bantam, 1971.

————. *In and Out of the Garbage Pail.* Toronto: Bantam, 1972.

Piaget, Jean. *The Psychology of Intelligence.* London: Routledge and Kegan Paul, 1950.

Polster, Erving, and Miriam Polster. *Gestalt Therapy Integrated.* New York: Vintage Books, 1973.

Shepard, Martin. *Fritz: An Intimate Portrait of Fritz Perls and Gestalt Therapy.* New York: E. P. Dutton, 1975.

Stafford-Clark, David. *What Freud Really Said.* New York: Schocken Books, 1971.

Stoller, Frederick H. *Encounter.* San Francisco: Jossey-Bass, 1970.

Wilber, Ken. *The Spectrum of Consciousness.* Wheaton, Illinois: Theosophical Publishing, 1977.

Wolman, Benjamin, ed. *The Handbook of Clinical Psychology.* New York: McGraw-Hill, 1965.

SOCIOLOGY

Berger, Peter, and Thomas Luckmann. *The Social Construction of Reality.* New York: Grove Press, 1966.

Campbell, Joseph. *The Hero with a Thousand Faces.* Princeton, N.J.: Princeton University Press, 1972.

Gottesfield, H., and G. Dozier. "Changes in Feelings of Powerlessness in a Community Action Program." *Psychological Reports,* vol. 24, no. 1, 1963.

Hampden-Turner, Charles. *Radical Man: The Process of Psycho-Social Development.* Garden City, N.Y.: Anchor Books, 1971.

Kuhn, Thomas S. *The Structure of Scientific Revolution.* Chicago: University of Chicago Press, 1962.

Leonard, George. *The Transformation.* New York: Delacorte, 1972.

McLuhan, Marshall, and Quentin Fiore. *The Medium Is the Massage.* New York: Random House, 1967.

Pearce, Joseph Chilton. *Exploring the Crack in the Cosmic Egg.* New York: Julian Press, 1974.

Thompson, William I. *At the Edge of History.* New York: Harper and Row, 1972.

SYSTEMS THEORY

Bertalanffy, Ludwig Von. *Robots, Men, and Minds: Psychology in the Modern World.* New York: George Braziller, 1967.

Maltz, Maxwell. *Psycho-Cybernetics.* New York: Pocket Books, 1969.

Satir, Virginia. *Peoplemaking.* Palo Alto, Calif.: Science and Behavior Books, 1972.

TRAINING AND DEVELOPMENT

Broadwell, Martin M., and P. Carol Broadwell. "Reaching for Rapport." *Training,* September 1987.

Feuer, Dale. "Training Budgets." *Training,* October 1986.

Gordon, Jack. "Where the Training Goes." *Training,* October 1986.

———. "The Woo Woo Factor." *Training,* May 1985.

Kinlaw, Dennis C., and Donna R. Christensen. "Management Education: The Wheat and the Chaff." *Training,* December 1986.

Kimmerling, George F. "Workers at Risk, Train Effectively." *Training and Development Journal,* April 1985.

Ludwig, John, and Diane Menendez. "Effective Communication Through Neurolinguistics." *Training and Development Journal,* March 1985.

O'Brien, Roger T. "Using Jung More (And Etching Him in Stone Less)." *Training,* May 1985.

Index

S

Picasso said that when he was twelve
he could draw like Raphael, but it had
taken him a lifetime to draw like a child.
Fine-tuning your brain for business
interactions is somewhat like that.